The Petigru Review

2014

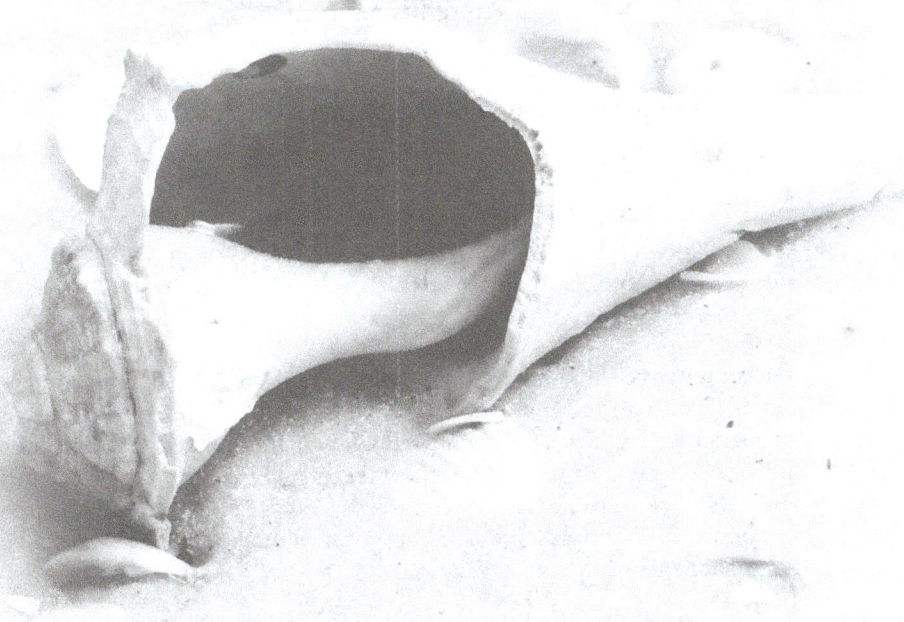

Volume 8

The Petigru Review – 2014
Volume 8

ISBN-13: 978-0-9714618-6-4
ISBN-10: 0971461864

The Petigru Review • 2014 • Volume 8

Printed and bound in the United States of America.

Published with support from the
South Carolina Arts Commission by:

South Carolina Writers' Workshop
4840 Forest Drive Suite 6-B: PMB 189
Columbia, SC 29206

Cover Photo: Barbara V. Evers
Back Cover Photo: Barbara V. Evers

Photo by Jayne Bowers

This project is funded in part by the Cultural Council of Richland and Lexington Counties and the South Carolina Arts Commission, which receives support from the National Endowment for the Arts and the John and Susan Bennett Memorial Arts Fund of the Coastal Community Foundation of SC.

Also sponsored by:
Fiction Addiction
1020A Woodruff Road
Greenville SC 29607
864.675.0540
www.fiction-addiction.com

CONTENTS

From the Editor

Trilby Plants

Photo by Linda Cookingham

Anyone who has ever walked on a beach and picked up a shell knows sea shells whisper secrets. If we listen we might hear the sounds of ancient oceans and the stories that have been told upon them. Stories first handed down in the oral tradition, disseminated across the land by travelers and over huge expanses of water by intrepid seafaring peoples. Oral traditions were eventually written, and with the advent of the printing press and safer sea travel, distributed to a world of readers.

Written words are precious: they preserve human history, scientific achievements, ideas, language. Words convey stories, poetry, truths. Stories and poetry show the human experience at its best and worst: truth and fiction, real and imagined.

The next time you pick up a seashell - literally or metaphorically - take a moment and truly listen. Think of this anthology as a seashell, bringing stories from disparate authors who share with you their love of storytelling.

CARRIE McCRAY MEMORIAL LITERARY AWARDS

Photo by Barbara V. Evers

FIRST CHAPTER OF A NOVEL

First Place

The Rake's Tale

Bettie Williams

Chapter 1

I'd rather be hanged."

Amelia Merritt, dowager Duchess of Winterbourne, did not take her son's declaration well. In fact, she gaped at him before sputtering, "You cannot be serious, Benedick."

"Ah, Mother," he replied, his generous mouth curving into a cocky grin. "You know me well enough to understand that I am indeed serious. I would rather be hanged than marry one of the twittering half-wits you daily toss into my path."

"They're not twittering half-wits. Lady Regina Hammond is the Earl of Weymouth's daughter and a diamond of the first water. She can speak French and Italian flawlessly, has amazing skill with the needle, and when she talks –"

"I find myself fighting off sleep. She is as much a diamond of the first water as I am the village vicar."

Sending her son a look of supreme annoyance, she continued, "What I was going to say – before being so rudely interrupted – was that when Lady Regina *talks*, there are always a multitude of suitors listening to every word she says."

"That is because she never shuts her mouth. Mother, just because a lady is courted by other men does not mean she will be enticing to me. It simply means the other men are idiots."

"You are entirely too fastidious on the matter. You are the only duke in all of London who is both unwed and young. You can have your pick of any girl around."

"You confuse me, madam. If indeed I have such a wide selection available to me, would not such an occasion call for fastidiousness?"

"The point is to actually *make* a choice, my son. I, myself, have introduced you to no less than five eligible debutantes this season alone, and you would have none of them," she huffed, taking a seat and motioning for her errant child to do the same.

Benedick took the chair across from her. He obviously did not care that his manners were less than *de rigeur*, however, as he leaned back in the seat with his legs splayed wide in a most ungentlemanly fashion. With one of his hands indolently resting along the back of her favorite chair, he was lounging more than sitting.

No doubt to irritate me more, Amelia thought. "That does not count the ladies from last season, all of whom are now married to *other* men."

"And I wish their husbands the best of luck. They will certainly need it. Admit it, Mother, there wasn't a rebel among them, and I'd have been bored within a week."

"*Rebel?* Are you looking to overthrow the government then?"

"No," he said. "But I don't wish to be married to someone too busy trying to be like everyone else to have a mind of her own."

"Rebel or not, I think it would be better to focus on ladies acceptable enough to be the next Duchess of Winterbourne. It is what I have been trying to do."

"Well, *acceptable* obviously does not mean to you what it does to me. The debutantes you have introduced me to are all made up of the same bits of annoying fluff, and I'm not interested in marrying any one of them. If I feel the need to be so tediously leg-shackled for all eternity, I shall commit a crime and turn myself over to the watch."

The smirk on his face only served to frustrate her further. If he hadn't towered a foot over her petite frame and weighed about two stone more than she did, she would have seriously considered taking him over her knee. It was at times like these that she thought a sound thrashing was just the thing to make him see reason.

"Nonetheless, the ladies I introduced to you to tonight were amiable and so accomplished. I found them rather – Why are you shaking your head at me like that?"

"*You* cannot be serious, Mother," he said, turning her former words against her.

"How can you say that? I found Lady Helen Chesterfield to be lovely. What is your issue with her?"

"Well, let's see," he said, removing his arm from the back of the chair as he leaned forward. "She's scared of her own shadow, spoke only two words together the whole evening, and fainted simply because old Lord Kensley dropped his quizzing glass in his soup bowl during dinner." He ticked off each reason with his fingers as he spoke. Then, his voice taking a sarcastic edge, Benedick announced, "You're quite right. She was absolutely perfect. My heart is all aflutter. Do you think I should propose right away or wait a bit for propriety's sake?"

She rolled her eyes. "At least you wouldn't have to worry about her talking constantly."

"You're entirely correct. However, I would spend my time *constantly* picking her up off the floor. No, thank you."

"And Miss Henley? Her mother was telling me of her daughter's amazing talent with watercolors. What is wrong with her?"

"She paints? That is indeed surprising as the woman's lack of common sense is trumped only by her lack of balance. She ran into three walls during the course of one evening because she was trying to bat those blasted eyelashes of hers at me instead of watching where she was going." He gave a bitter smile. "*I think not.*"

"And Lady Mary Pennington? What of her? I was told she loves to read. And, since I hardly ever see you without your head in a book, I would say she would suit you quite well." She nodded regally, sure she had him cornered this time.

He expelled a harsh breath. "I do not count those serialized Gothic novels that are all the crack these days as true reading. Lady Mary is an ignorant twit. She thought Shakespeare was some kind of weapon, for God's sake."

Amelia pursed her lips to stifle a laugh. Patting her graying, blonde hair, she sat up straighter, trying to regain her composure. It would not do any good for him to know he'd amused her. Benedick would only see it as a win for his side of the argument, and she couldn't have that. Time to go at this from another angle.

"My son, as the Duke of Winterbourne, you must marry and provide an heir for the title. It's your duty. You have run from your responsibilities long enough."

"Run, is it?" he said, sitting up in his chair, his relaxed stance gone. The half-smile on his face seemed forced for the sake of politeness rather than an expression of happiness. "I have hardly spent the last eight years sitting on my laurels."

"I agree, but now that you are about to turn thirty, you must concede marriage is your next logical step."

His aquamarine eyes flared in anger. "We have had this discussion before, Mother. I believe it was after my father's funeral when you told me the family coffers were empty and it was my *duty* to marry a rich heiress so they might be filled again. I believe you called it the *next logical step*. Am I correct?"

"Yes, but – "

He interrupted her. "Yet, instead of marrying an heiress, I took what *I* considered to be the next logical step and went to see my steward and clerk. I then dedicated myself to turning around the management of the estates, which had been all but neglected by my father as well as his father before him. I uncovered the former steward's embezzlement of estate profits, and, after turning the brigand over to the proper authorities, I not only hired a new steward, but also implemented modern, more efficient ways of running the estates so we might receive the most possible income from them."

"Your father was never good with financial matters," she grumbled, as if that excused anything.

Benedick continued as though he hadn't heard her. "Then, after taking the profit earned from the estates and making a few sound investments, I turned what was once an almost empty account into a mass of great wealth. We are now more financially sound than old Damien Merritt was when he was first granted the title in 1642. Is that not also correct?"

Amelia took a moment to answer. She didn't like where this was going. "Yes."

"Then, I believe you were wrong to say that I have been running away from my responsibilities. To my way of thinking, I have been doing little else all this time but seeing to my duties to this title. Therefore, would it be correct for me to say that what you assume is the *next logical step* for me is not always so?"

Instead of answering, she let her son see the look of total exasperation on her face. He was too clever for his own good. If he had not been born the heir to a dukedom, he could have been a wonderful barrister. No one else she knew could make a more logical, concise argument. But, alas, that was not to be.

He had always been a determined rascal, whose charm, wit, and charisma – if he felt inclined to display them – could yield him anything he wanted. Hadn't he been the one to talk the old stable master into letting him ride the new, barely broken stallion his father had purposefully forbidden him to go near? In the end, he'd not only charmed the stable master, but the horse as well. He'd even talked his father out of taking the strap to him. Oh yes, Benedick had a persuasive way, all right. A trait received from her, she considered wryly.

His father's death had brought out a new side to her son. He had become serious, straitlaced, and responsible, seeming to leave behind his uninhibited ways. Benedick took to the duties of his title with a rigid ferocity that had left her stunned at times, and she worried the darling rascal he had once been might be gone forever. It was only on occasions like this she could still see bits of it peeking out from behind his daily mask of stoic propriety.

He was certainly an odd mixture. He was every inch the respectable, English gentleman, but also had an annoying habit of thwarting tradition at times. It was a custom in the Merritt family that the oldest son married by his twenty-fifth birthday. However, Benedick seemed inclined to keep his bachelor's existence on into his thirties. Also, he hadn't taken his rightful place in society. Instead, he went out into the *ton* but rarely and seemed happier running the estates and staying in the country. From the way he was going, she would be dead in her grave before he even started *thinking* about getting a wife.

He was right about one thing, though. This was not the first time they'd had this discussion. It was a merry battle they'd been waging for years. When he was in town, she would set up small dinner parties, cajole him into attending a society ball, or any other underhanded trick she could think of just to throw him into the paths of eligible ladies. When he could not get out of attending, he would arrive, show the bare minimum of courtesy to the debutantes as well as their mothers and leave as unmarried as always.

It was enough to make her want to pull out every hair in her head. Later, they would retire to the drawing room to debate the issue until she would finally give up and bid him good night. The next morning, she would arise with a new plan and the cycle would start again. So far, this evening was turning out no differently. But the night was not over yet. This time her plan was too perfect, too foolproof. If luck was on her side, she would see her son espoused by this time next year with – dare she hope? – an heir on the way. The thing to do now was bait the hook and wait for the fish to bite.

"You do not mean to marry at all then?"

"That's not what I meant. I'm simply saying when the time comes, I will find my own wife," Benedick said.

"What qualities do you seek?"

He eyed her with suspicion. "I would no more tell you that than I would ride my horse in Hyde Park, unclothed. Just understand constantly pushing these women at me is not going to help me in this endeavor."

"So, you *are* looking?"

"I'm not interested in settling down anytime soon. I have too much else I would like to do before I'm charged with the heavy burden of a wife."

"A wife is not a burden if you love her. In fact, you could share the burdens you already have with her. She could be your partner. I could find that woman for you if you would only tell me what qualities you most esteem."

"Mother," he said, releasing another pent up breath of frustration, "love is not an emotion I'm interested in finding. When I choose to marry, I will decide based on several areas of compatibility, keeping in mind my needs for my life. I will not have just any inane lady as the next Duchess of Winterbourne. She will not be like all of these other women, who chatter on nonstop about fashion, gossip, and frippery. And that marriage will not be arranged by you. In any case, how can you dare speak of love and partnership in marriage when, in the beginning, you wanted me wed for fortune's sake?"

"How was I to know I had a son with a mind for commerce? I have no doubt that particular sentiment would send some of the previous dukes of Winterbourne spinning in their graves, but I, for one, couldn't be happier about your talent. None of that matters now because we are, as you say, financially sound. This time, I'm talking about a life partner for you. Not an heiress, not a business arrangement, but a true, loving wife."

"When the time comes, I will wed for more logical and practical reasons. I have no need to find myself turning into an imbecile over a female because of *love*. As far as I am concerned, the emotion does not exist."

"I would have you know that your father and I had a marriage arranged by our parents, and we were quite happy. I fell in love with him the moment I saw him riding his stallion across my father's country estate. He'd come to meet me and make our betrothal official. He looked so dashing and cavalier that I thought him to be my very own knight in shining armor." She was seeing it all inside her head, and she smiled at the image, not caring that her voice had taken on a strange tone, almost dreamlike in quality.

"'Knight in shining armor'? You always told me Father toppled off of his horse, and you had to help him up."

"I did," she said. "Yet, for the three minutes he was on that stallion, he was my knight. His falling off only made it all the better. I got to rescue him. Your father always said that when he saw me running to help him, he fell in love with me." She sighed. "Love is what got us through. We were happy, and that is all I want for you. My parents knew I would do well with Edmund, and they were quite right. Who knows a child better than his parent?" Grief over the thought of her dead husband clogged her throat, causing her words to come out slightly hoarse.

Benedick moved next to her on the settee and took her hand. He wiped away the tears spilling from her eyes with his other hand, and she could see how her grief pained him. It had always affected him so. She almost felt guilty over what she was going to do to him. *Almost.*

"Mother, I did not mean to offend you by implying your marriage was not one based on love or that you did not know me well. Still, as there are many marriages which work out as yours did, there are just as many that turn out quite the opposite. I will put it this way if it makes you feel better: I do not believe it is my lot in life to find love in marriage. I know my duty, nonetheless, and when the time comes, I will take a wife. I expect we will get on quite amiably. I am content with that."

She squeezed his hand. "Then I feel sorry for you, my boy."

"Sorry enough to quit this marriage discussion for good?"

"No," she said, taking a deep breath. "But I am willing to come to a compromise."

He pursed his lips. "What type of compromise?"

"I will leave the choosing of your bride in your hands …." She let her words trail off and looked down so that he wouldn't see the smile she was trying to hold in.

"And what must I do in return?"

"Attend a party."

Benedick's mind raced. If he agreed to attend one event, she would leave off of her persistent need to see him wed. It would be nice to visit his mother's home without having to dodge eligible females. It would be lovely to have a more sedate, pleasant time with her instead of the same old battle where he must constantly be on his toes.

He didn't relish attending social events. Being a part of the *ton* was more a tedious burden than any kind of privilege. It would be worth attending some idiotic ball to be free forever. Still, suspicion loomed.

It couldn't be that easy, he told himself. It was never this easy with her. There has to be a catch. There's always a catch.

"Let me see if I have this correct in my mind," he said. "I attend this one event, and, in exchange, you will forever leave off your persistent need to see me wed?"

"There are a few conditions."

"Of course there are," he said, preparing himself for battle. He was perched on the edge of his seat. "Go ahead."

"First, you must promise to stay until the festivities are over. You may not show up for a few minutes and leave soon after."

He nodded. "Go on."

"Second, you must take part in the revelries. You may not hide in the library the whole time or any other such nonsense."

"Anything else? I assume you will be attending this affair to gauge my progress?"

"No, I trust you to keep your word once you've given it. Although, there is a third condition."

"I see. Go on."

"You must ask to be introduced to two ladies with whom you do not currently claim an acquaintance and attempt a conversation with them lasting no less than fifteen minutes. After your conversation, if you find them not to your liking, you may leave them be."

He couldn't believe his luck. There had to be more to this scheme of hers. What his mother asked was bothersome, but hardly beyond his capabilities. "And this is all I must agree to?"

"Yes," she said, demurely. "Will you agree?"

"Completely. You have my word of honor."

"Excellent," she said. She kissed his cheek, bid him good-night, and started to leave the room. She'd almost made it to the door before his next question stopped her.

"Which event will I be attending?"

When his mother turned back to look at him, he was startled to see the impish smirk.

"The Hamilton Garden Party," she said. "I have already procured you an invitation. It will be sent over to your lodgings tomorrow."

She was so sure he would agree that she'd already gotten the invitation? Her overconfidence was not going to make her matchmaking plans any more successful this time than they had been previously. The Duke of Winterbourne would leave the Hamilton Garden Party just as unattached as when he arrived.

Benedick got to his feet, running the name of the event through his mind. Why did it sound so familiar? Shaking his head after a moment, he decided it was unimportant. It wasn't usual for him to keep up with every event on the social calendar. He could ask Conrad about it tomorrow. His closest friend knew everything about the goings-on of the *ton*.

He whistled as he took his things from the butler, hardly able to believe how it had all worked out. Attend one party and he would at last be free of his mother's constant manipulations. It was too wonderful an idea to fully accept. Freedom, finally.

It was going to be heaven.

BETTIE WILLIAMS has been an author of novels, short stories, and some really bad poetry for over twenty years. She's been published in the *Petigru Review, USCA's Broken Ink* and a few anthologies presented through the Maryland Writer's Association. Bettie holds bachelor's degrees in communications as well as English from USCA. When she isn't writing, Bettie enjoys obsessing over Jane Austen and William Shakespeare, beating every person she knows at Scattergories and having debates with herself that she has no hope of winning. Bettie makes her home in North Augusta, SC and has been employed at Georgia Regents University since 2010.

FIRST CHAPTER OF A NOVEL

Second Place

Whispers from the Past

Mary Edelson

Chapter One

The spine was broken, the cover was warped, and the brittle pages smelled of mold and dust. In other words, it was perfect. Most people would walk right past it, or worse yet, toss it in the trash can, but not me. I'm odd that way. I prefer old books – worn and faded with creases down the middle and battered edges. They have a story to tell, and I've loved a good story as long as I can remember.

I tucked the volume under my arm and ventured farther into the stall, not really looking for anything in particular. But then, I rarely was. Mostly I loved puttering through the remnants of other people's lives. Things that had once been family treasures. Things that would whisper to you if you only stopped talking and running hell bent for leather through life and listened.

The antique mall was housed in an old mill, and the floor was uneven and bumpy. Every nook and cranny was crammed with tea pots, crystal goblets, brass and silver-plated candle sticks, mismatched cups and saucers and stacks of yellowed newspapers and old postcards. Fractured light sifted through the grimy windows, reflecting off tarnished silver and dirty cut glass. I took a deep breath, inhaling a hundred years of hopes and dreams and triumphs and sorrows.

I stepped over a box of chipped china and bits of yellow lace and found the wedding picture half-buried under a broken toaster and a pile of old pamphlets and magazines. The bride wore a simple gown without any frills. The kind I'd have chosen. No hideous ruffles or piles of lace or bows. A long strand of pearls was her only adornment. The groom stood beside her, one hand on her shoulder. Possessive or protective, I couldn't tell. The bride's mouth was curved in a playful smile, as if she knew a secret and couldn't wait to share it.

"Check out the wedding dress." The shop owner tucked a loose strand of hair behind her ear and pointed at the bride. "Reminds me of my grandmother. She was a flapper, too."

I looked down at the picture, again. Now that she mentioned it, the bride's dress did resemble a flapper's. Drop waist. Hemline rakishly high, somewhere around mid-calf.

I flipped it over. *New York, 1923. Julia and Max's wedding* was penned across the bottom in faded ornate script.

"There's another one here somewhere." She reached onto a shelf and pulled down a stack of pictures, riffling through until she found a second photo. This one showed four people. The same bride and groom with two other people. The maid of honor and the bride looked like twins, except she was more conservatively dressed.

"That's what they called a Gibson Girl dress." She grinned. "Guess they didn't see eye to eye on things."

The best man stood a few steps away from the groom. His

face was too narrow and his nose too large to be handsome, but there was something in his expression that made him appealing. A man you could trust. A man you wanted to be your friend.

A sudden and inexplicable ache filled my chest, pushing the breath from my lungs. I had no idea who these people were, but I desperately wanted to know. I wanted to know their story and I wanted, deep in my bones, to somehow be connected. To have their story be mine.

"They're perfect," I said, tracing a finger along the front of the photo.

"Want me to take them up front for you? So you can keep looking around?" She smiled and held out a hand.

"It's all right," I said. "I'm done anyway." I clutched the pictures. For some strange reason, I was loath to let go of them, even for a few moments.

What in the world had gotten into me? I certainly had no interest in weddings, whatever the vintage. Two weeks ago, I'd ended an eighteen-month on-again-off-again relationship and watched Sid, the man I thought I'd loved, haul ass into the sunset.

"Suit yourself." The owner shrugged and led the way to the front of the store.

I scooted past a rickety washstand loaded down with assorted cut glass pitchers and dusty mason jars. As I approached the register, I came face-to-face with a wicker baby carriage. The sight of it jarred an unpleasant feeling in my gut, one I'd been trying to bury for the past few days. For the umpteenth time, I did a mental calculation and came up with the same answer. I was three and a half weeks late. My hand skimmed over my flat belly.

"You're sure that's it?" She said. "I bought a boxful of things at an estate sale a month or so ago. Some interesting pieces of jewelry and a some really charming hats."

"Not today." I forced a smile to my face. My lips felt like

wood. "I've got a ton of errands to do."

I pulled out my cell phone and glanced at the time, trying to ignore the mass of weevils I seemed to have swallowed. There was nothing to do but face the facts, once and for all. I'd stop at CVS on the way home and pick up a home pregnancy test. The thought made me wobble in my tracks.

I had trouble opening the box. Given my history, that wasn't unreasonable. A month before her high school graduation, my mother hemorrhaged to death while giving birth, splattering blood all over the grime encrusted black-and-white tiles in the ladies room at Lou Ella's Mini-Mart off Tompkins Road. The girl working the graveyard shift heard my squalls and called 9-1-1, but my mother was already dead.

I ripped the cellophane wrapper off the pregnancy test. With all the advances in modern technology, did I really have to pee on a plastic stick to see if I was pregnant? My hands were trembling, and I was lucky to hit the window on the stupid wand. I sat on the edge of the tub and waited, knowing it was a waste of time. Deep inside, I already knew the answer. When the plus sign popped into view, I dropped it in the trash, leaned over the commode and threw up.

I'd spent my adult life running from my mother's legacy, determined not to end up like her. And here I was. Unmarried and pregnant.

I sat up straight, pushing my hair out of my eyes.

Not like her. There was a world of difference between us. I was an adult. Twenty-six years old. I had a job and an apartment and I sure as hell wasn't going to have my baby on a filthy bathroom floor.

My baby?

Who was I kidding? What did I know about being a mother? I hadn't even had one. And since my mother died without ever divulging my father's identity, I hadn't had a father, either. What I did have was a lifetime of blundering through a world designed for Hallmark families. I knew firsthand what it was like to sit alone through elementary school celebrations. Muffins for Mom. Doughnuts for Dad.

My legs were shaking so badly it was hard to stand, but I managed to rinse my mouth and then wash my face. I stared at my reflection in the mirror.

Way to go, Emma.

I fumbled for my cell phone. What time was it in Iraq? Would Sid care? He'd taken the job with a civilian contractor without discussing it with me and left without a backward glance.

"You have problems with commitment," he'd said. "I'm done wasting my time."

I hadn't heard a word from him since he'd bolted. I shoved the phone back into my pocket.

Just how was I supposed to tell him, anyway? It didn't exactly seem like the kind of news to drop on him in a text.

Umm, no big deal but thought you might want to know you left something behind ....

Abortion. Adoption. Single motherhood. Reconciling with Sid. The choices swirled around my head like leaves in an autumn squall. I closed my eyes and gripped the edge of the sink. In spite of my natural inclination to believe I could force any situation to turn out the way I intended it to – through brute force or strength of will or natural cussedness – in this case I wasn't so sure a happy ending was in the cards.

I stumbled out of the bathroom and scooped my keys out of the bowl on the counter. Everyone has a different method of dealing with stress. Some people exercise. Some turn to alcohol. I seek solace in books.

I lived in an apartment above the second-hand bookstore I managed. It was an hour past closing. The perfect refuge. I unlocked the door and switched on the lights.

I had a box of books I'd bought the previous weekend I hadn't dealt with yet. I moved to the back of the store and started unloading them, feeling my muscles relax and my gut untangle after a few minutes of peace and solitude. I flipped through the pages of a paperback copy of *The Awakening*. Minimal damage. Whoever'd owned it before had probably never read it. A shame. I stacked it on top of a collection of Flannery O'Connor short stories to shelve in the Southern Women's Lit section.

Although Sid did not share my passion for books, he did read. Mostly nonfiction. History. Psychology. Memoirs. He had an opinion on nearly every subject. If I told him I was pregnant, I knew what his solution would be.

The only problem was, he'd already asked me once, when I wasn't pregnant, and I'd said no. Marrying him for the sake of a baby seemed a bit last century. Not fair to me or Sid.

I pulled another book from the box. A treatise on Pearl Harbor. I slipped it into the history pile. Even if I wanted to marry him, he wasn't exactly available at the moment. He'd signed a year contract providing security to some private corporation in Iraq. Dangerous but lucrative. He sprang it on me one night after dinner. No discussion. No warning. Just an ultimatum.

"Marry me or I take the job."

I was pretty sure I loved Sid, but I wasn't the type to be bullied into anything. I wasn't ready for marriage, and he wasn't willing to compromise.

I sorted the remaining books into stacks and carried them to the appropriate sections of the store. My eye caught a book about pregnancy. I picked it up and thumbed through it. There was a section that described calculating the due date. I pulled out my cell phone and clicked on the calendar. According to the book, I would be due in mid-December.

One glance at the calendar told me exactly when we'd conceived. A Friday night two months earlier, a horrendous rain storm knocked out all the power. Nothing more romantic than huddling under blankets, eating leftover Chinese food by candlelight. The fact that Sid was out of condoms was a minor detail at the time.

The memory sent a palpable ache through my chest. A hole that wasn't easy to fill. I could see Sid, his blond curls falling in soft tangles around his face. His easy grin. One front tooth a little chipped from an incident with a basketball when he'd been ten.

I pulled out my phone. Started a text message. Deleted it. What in the world could I possibly say? I'd already turned down his marriage proposal. I couldn't say yes now just because I was pregnant and scared. If I really loved him, I would have said yes the first time. But if I didn't love him, why did it hurt so badly?

I heard the lock on the front door click open. Only one other person had a key.

"I saw the light was on." Sylvia's heels clicked against the tile floor. "I was coming to bring you some soup. You haven't been eating right since …." She let the rest of the sentence trail off. "You look awful." She peered at me in the dim light. "And what are you doing down here this late? On your day off?"

I wanted nothing more than to bury myself in her arms and cry on her shoulders. Sylvia was more than my boss. She was more than a friend. She was the mother I'd never had. I'd always confided in her, but this time, as much as I wanted to tell her everything, the words stuck in my throat.

I knew Sylvia's deepest sorrows, too. She'd lost five babies. She and her husband had been desperate to have a family but one miscarriage after another had crushed every hope. In the end, they'd given up. He'd died six years ago.

I couldn't confide in her. Not while I might choose to voluntarily terminate the pregnancy.

"Just trying to get some of these books put up before tomorrow," I said. I brushed my hands against my jeans.

"Give him time," she said. "It hasn't been that long."

I forced a smile. Better that she should think I was distraught over Sid than she should know the truth.

She stepped toward me and kissed my cheek. "Let's go upstairs before the soup gets cold."

I followed her upstairs and into the kitchen.

I rubbed my belly. Silly, really. It was no different than it had been two hours ago. Before I'd known. And it couldn't be more than a few cells that had taken up residence in my uterus. Like a cyst. Easily removed. Wasn't that the best solution? I would call Planned Parenthood first thing in the morning. Find out all the details. I needed information and then I could make a decision. And if I decided to terminate, Sid never needed to know.

Sylvia ladled soup into a bowl and set it in front of me.

"I tried a new recipe today," she said. "A mixed apple-berry strudel. I brought you a piece for dessert."

"You really are worried." I smiled at her over the steam from my soup.

I'd met Sylvia the summer after my second year in college. I was almost out of money and desperate for a job and cheaper accommodations. I ducked into her bakery to avoid getting drenched in a sudden rainstorm. It was almost closing and we struck up a conversation. Over a piece of her apple strudel, I unloaded my problems.

"Everything happens for a reason," she said.

It turned out she owned the building. The downstairs housed her bakery and another business. Elaine's Eclectic Entities.

"There's an apartment upstairs," she said. "It's in pretty bad shape and it's been vacant for years. My husband was always planning to fix it up but something always came up, and he died before he ever got around to it."

"I'm sorry."

She smiled and wiped the counter. "Thank you. But the point is, if you don't mind a fixer-upper …."

In the end, she paid for the paint, and I did the work. Two months later, by the start of my junior year, I had a new apartment and the best landlady in the world. She gave me all the day-old bread and muffins that hadn't sold, and I figured if I didn't put her out of business eating all the profits, I was going to gain fifty pounds.

"How's the soup?" Sylvia pulled me out of my reverie.

"Delicious. As always." I made an appreciative smacking noise and wiped my lips. In truth, I'd barely tasted it. "I bought a book today." I changed the subject. "It needs some work but I thought it would be perfect for my next attempt with Gustav." I'd met a bookbinder a year ago and he was teaching me his craft.

"Good. A distraction is exactly what you need. Something to keep you busy." She whisked the soup bowl away and plopped a plate in front of me.

"Not yet," she said when I started to take a bite. She rummaged in the refrigerator for whipped cream. "Who's that good-looking man I saw you talking to in the store yesterday?" she said, spooning a dollop of cream the size of a baseball on my dessert.

"He's a TA at VCU. He's going to teach a weekly seminar after we close on Wednesday nights. Somewhere between eight and ten students. I told him you'd provide coffee and dessert."

Four years ago, Elaine's Eclectics went belly up. After the rooms stayed empty for a few months, I talked Sylvia into trying her hand with a used bookstore. She opened No Page Unturned a year and a half later and hired me as the manager. We knocked out the connecting wall and added some decorative columns to separate the bookstore from the bakery.

On the bookstore side, I filled the front room with comfy chairs and colorful rugs. Free wi-fi and free coffee. The back room was lined with floor to ceiling bookshelves and an honest-to-goodness antique rolling ladder.

My cell phone rang, and I nearly knocked the chair over leaping for it. Sylvia watched me but I shook my head when I saw the caller ID. "It's not Sid," I said.

I recognized the number, even though I hadn't seen it in years – Stanley Jenkins, my grandfather's best friend. I hesitated, considered ignoring the call, but in the end, habit took over and I answered it.

"It's not a good time, Stanley."

"You're breaking my heart. Get your sorry ass home," he said. Stanley Jenkins never minced words, but his typical king-of-the-sandpile manner failed miserably this time. He sounded like he'd swallowed a mouthful of gravel. "Your granddad needs you."

"Like he needs a hole in his head." I tucked the phone against my cheek and mouthed "sorry" to Sylvia. "It's been a long day. Can we discuss this some other time?"

"Em –"

"Granddad doesn't need anyone, Stanley. He never has. Nice try, but –"

"He's in the hospital."

"What did he break this time?" Granddad was a career soldier. He'd fought in two wars and came through unscathed. He might be approaching eighty-five, but the thought that he was mortal like the rest of us never crossed my mind. He was a fixture. A constant that would never disappear. I picked up my coffee cup and took a sip.

"He had a stroke."

Outside, a car alarm pierced the silence.

"The doctors don't know if he'll make it through the night."

I reached out to put my cup on the table and bumped the edge. The coffee splattered everywhere, a swirling lake of scalding liquid engulfing my shoes, the chair, the floor.

MARY EDELSON grew up in Pennsylvania but fled south to attend the University of Virginia and never looked back. She's published three short stories in *The Petigru Review* and has had two others named to the short list of finalists in the Faulkner-Wisdom Contest. Her first novel, *Mourning's Golden Mist*, is in the hands of her agent, Kevan Lyon. She is currently working on her second, *Whispers From the Past*. She lives in Lexington with her husband and four children. When not at work or writing, you can find her poking around dusty antique shops or out riding her horse.

FIRST
CHAPTER OF
A NOVEL
Honorable Mention

Ruby Sky
Wendy C. Oglesby

BY THE LIGHT OF THE MOON
Deacon Wade

4 AM

I'm not sure if it's the pounding or the shouting that wakes me. My eyes pop open, but my head's about as clear as mud, and I'm shivering hard enough to hurt, though the wheezing window unit struggles to keep the temperature in here under eighty.

I roll over and bury my face in the sofa, panting the left-behind stink of Irena Little's beloved Marlboros, waiting for my brain to engage. My tee shirt clings to me like I've been swimming instead of dozing on this spongy couch in the Little Bit of Heaven Motel office, and my clammy skin crawls like daddy longleg spiders are walking across me. A chalky anise taste coats my mouth. All are tell tale signs that I have been dreaming *the dream*.

What *the dream* is, I couldn't tell you. I don't remember my dreams. Not a one. Haven't since I was nineteen and ignorant as dirt. But I know the residue of this particular dream like the back of my hand.

The guy at the door hollers again, shouting he's from next door, from the Mermaid Cove, the latest and greatest new resort to open here in the Red Neck Riviera, otherwise known as Myrtle Beach, South Carolina. Then, he calls out his name like somebody's supposed to care, and suddenly, I do.

Tom Jones.

His name hits me like a two by four. I scramble to my feet as my throat closes up like I've swallowed a load of dirty socks. I limp for the door, thinking for the first time in a long time about another Tom Jones. The one who killed my mother.

We heard that blame name everywhere for years after it happened because the famous Tom Jones was in his heyday back then, and you couldn't turn on the radio without hearing that name and his songs. We stopped listening in the car because my sister Ruby cried every time he came on, but nothing could stop other kids from razzing us about it. Trust me. Having your mamma killed by someone who sounds famous is the rotten cherry on a shit sundae.

I'm not a man who dwells on the past so it surprises me how quickly this ancient history rushes back and how much that name out of the blue shocks, like my fingers are jammed into a light socket instead of the white plastic blinds covering the office door. I squint between the slats at the trim, crew cut Tom Jones outside. He doesn't look a thing like famous Tom or my mother's killer. That Tom Jones was a fat, old fuck whose heart blew a gasket as he was driving his white Buick Electra past our house. His tank-on-wheels took out our mailbox and then my mother, who was down on her knees behind it planting yellow tulip bulbs.

Everything happens for a reason, they say. God moves in mysterious ways. Maybe so, but all I know for sure is that the socks in my throat have hardened into a hot, solid lump I can't swallow away to save my life. Now it's my Grandma Mag in my mind's eye I see, swinging a hoe at the green shoots that poked up around the mailbox the March after my mother died.

When the man outside shouts again, I realize I haven't said a word to him yet.

"Open up. I need to talk to you." Tom has discovered the buzzer and he leans long and hard on it to make his point.

"Lay off that buzzer. I hear you." If this idiot wakes Irena, I will kick his ass. I glance over my shoulder at the stairs to the second floor, holding my breath. It's still dark at the top. Some nights, nothing will wake Irena Little, the Bit's owner. Godzilla could march out of the ocean howling bloody murder, and she wouldn't twitch. But other nights, the sound of the waves keeps her up. I never know how the nights … or the days will play out. Not any more.

I turn the lock and step outside. Tom Jones is all decked out in a serious, navy blue uniform with some kind of badge on his chest. He's dressed to fool our drunk and disorderly tourists into thinking he's a real cop with real authority. His outfit sets my teeth on edge as he repeats his god-awful name and who he works for yet again. I ignore the palm he sticks out. I'm not shaking any Tom Jones' hand, but I bark my particulars – Deacon Wade with the Little Bit of Heaven – back at him and ask what the hell he wants this time of night.

Jones draws back his palm. "I'm sorry to get you up, but we got ourselves a problem that can't wait."

"A problem? You're kidding." I gape at this silly fool. What in the world does Tom here expect? It's Memorial Day Weekend. Everybody in Myrtle Beach knows this weekend is one giant tsunami of trouble with every black biker in America rolling in for the annual Atlantic Beach Rally and a legion of drunk teenagers piling in on top of them as the high schools graduate their classes. It's a rite-of-passage, a pilgrimage to the holy Grand Strand, when you graduate anything in the Carolinas. Come Saturday, there won't be an empty room from Calabash to Georgetown, and the rough holiday crowd will be well on its way to driving everyone from the cops to the strippers crazy. This nitwit here and his bosses are about to get an education. Welcome to Memorial Day Weekend at the Grand Strand.

Jones scowls. He knows contempt when he sees it. "Look, I'm doing you a favor coming over here. Are you going to help me solve this problem or not?"

I cross my arms and let him stew. Jones waits. I sigh and roll my eyes, but I know a bulldog when I see one. "All right. Let's get this over with. What is this big problem that *we* have?"

Tom warns me I better cut my shitty attitude or he'll call the police and let them deal with the problem. "I came over here first trying to be a good neighbor."

Good neighbor, my ass. He's come over here because he knows the cops won't. This weekend, only major mayhem commands their attention, and I don't hear any gunfire or explosions at the moment. In this sticky, pre-dawn darkness the full moon is all that's out on Ocean Boulevard. A few hours ago Myrtle's main drag snarled with bikes and cars lined up bumper to bumper as far as I could see in both directions. The sidewalks overflowed with people, the whole night alive and throbbing with noise. Things change so fast around here I can't keep up, though my girlfriend April says that's because I don't want to.

Jones snaps his fingers. "Hey! Are you listening to me? What are you going to do?"

He sounds like April. *What are you going to do, Deacon? You're forty years old. When are you going to stop wasting your potential?* I grimace. I'd rather talk to Jones than think about that. "What am I going to do about what?" I ask him.

"These girls skinny dipping in your pool." Jones shoves his hands into his pockets and shakes his head. He's had it.

So have I. "You're over here this time of night because some-one is skinny-dipping in *our* pool? That's your idea of *big trouble*? Buddy, you are going to have one long weekend."

"Fine then. I'll call the cops, and they can arrest these girls for indecent exposure and wake up everyone else staying at this dump in the process. I thought I'd give you a chance to take care of this yourself and avoid a big commotion, but whatever. You ought to be ashamed. I've seen your mother. She's not well. But since you insist on turning this into a big to-do, you got it." He stomps towards the steps that go down to the street.

"Irena's not my mother."

"Thank God. I'd hate to think that old woman was depend-ing on you."

I bit my lip. I've got the shivers again. What if I'm wrong and Myrtle's finest do respond when called by important places like the Mermaid Cove? The last thing in the world I want tonight – any time – is an encounter with cops. "Hold on, Jones. What do our naked girls have to do with you people anyway?"

Jones slows, but doesn't stop.

"Come on back, Jones. You're right. You're right. We don't need to get the police involved."

The second "you're right" does the trick. Jones turns and fills me in on the story as he comes back over. Two boys staying at the Mermaid spied the skinny dippers from their balcony and grabbed their daddy's new binoculars to get a better look. When their mamma caught them, they dropped dad's expensive toy over the railing.

"The parents are royally pissed," Jones says. "They want these 'little sluts,' as the mamma phrased it, out of their little angels' sight, and 'taught a hard lesson' about flashing their tits in public." Jones eyes dart toward his shoes and he shuffles around. "They also expect somebody to pay for the binoculars." He clears his throat.

"My manager says you need to give us $500 to cover that."

I laugh so hard I fart. "Tell your boss he's should come over here in the morning and talk to Mrs. Little's son about that. He'll be here around ten." I ask Jones if he'll help me run the girls out of the pool. His dang ugly uniform may come in handy for this project.

Jones grins. "No problem. That's the least I can do." It appears he likes young titties, too.

I tell him to come on in while I get my shoes. I can feel his eyes getting big behind me as I scoot around the walnut desk we use as a check-in counter. The sign on the desk identifies this space as the Little Bit of Heaven office, but mostly, this room is Irena's parlor and the rest of this house is her home. The motel proper squats out back.

Jones whistles. "This is a real unusual setup you got here."

"What do you mean by that?" I pretend to bristle as I extract my flip-flops from the couch cushions.

"No offense. I meant you don't see a house with a motel in the backyard much. That's all."

I smile. That's not what he means at all. He' talking about this crazy room. Irena's parlor befuddles everybody. I don't know if it's the suit of armor, the polar bear rug or the life-sized mural of James Brown that startles folks the most. No one's prepared for this interior because the outside of Irena's place looks like your run-of-the-mill beach rambler, what they call "shabby chic" at Pawley's Island, except the shabby is a little more pronounced around here.

White asbestos shingles stained the color of steamed oysters cover the house. Everywhere you look, there's a porch or desk hanging off, and that, combined with the fact the house sits twenty feet above the ground on thick wooden pillars, makes it appear bigger than it actually is. Irena parks her silver 1980 Caddy on one side of the cement pad underneath the house. My old Charger sits on the other side, and at the far end in the shadows, there's the guest suite that I call home. I moved in the same year as the Caddy.

Jones has worked his way over to the picture window. Pale silk drapes spotted from smoke and water stains cover the glass at the moment, but in the mornings, before I bring Irena down, I open these curtains and reveal the view – half a football field of green grass that gives way at the dune line to shimmering sea oats and beyond, Myrtle's famous white sand and surf.

"This could be a real nice house with a little fixing up," Jones says.

"The land is what's valuable."

"You're right about that the way this town is growing. She got any offers?"

Sharp yips from the upstairs landing save me the pain of answering. "Watch it, Jones. She bites," I say as Irena's black Chihuahua Miss Chiquita blows down the steps.

Damn it to hell. Irena's up for sure.

I lunge towards the stairs and sure enough, there she is, teetering at the top, clutching the walker that is almost tall as she is. She's still vain about her hair, and it hangs around her shoulders, thin, but coal black – the way she likes it – and brittle as glass from my rotten dye jobs. When she was in her prime, people mistook her for Elizabeth Taylor, or so I've been told more than once.

"What are you doing out of bed, lady?" I say.

"Miss Chiquita needs to pee." Irena's voice is gaunt as her arms. It hurts my heart to hear her talk. It seems like yesterday I could hear her bellowing for me over the roar of a lawn mower. Now, she strings her words like pearls with tight, knotty gasps between each one.

"Where's your oxygen? Shit, Irena." She's pale as my khakis.

I scoop her up. "You know better than to get up by yourself." In the bedroom, I tuck her into the hospital bed and attach the oxygen line to her nose. She needs the oxygen all the time now.

"Stop fiddling with me," she says. "I can do that myself. What's going on downstairs? Such a racket."

"Nothing important." I turn the tank valve up a notch and tell myself it's the light that makes her look so fragile. She's cool to my touch and almost translucent.

"Stop looking at me like that. I know I am no sight to see."

"You look good for an old lady."

"Liar." She smacks her smoky lips, but she likes a compliment.

Her rough breathing softens enough that I can muster a smile. I tuck a blanket around her and explain about the skinny dippers. "I'm fixing to go and run them out of the pool."

Irena closes her eyes. "How am I so tired when I do nothing?"

"I wish you wouldn't get up by yourself. That's why I got the horn." I tap the silver bike horn clamped to the rail of the bed. "You need something, squeeze that thing, and I'll come running." I reach to check her pulse, but she twists her wrist away.

"You are like a blowfly, I swear. Enough with this hovering. I am not a corpse yet." She mutters something else in her native Romany.

"You aren't cussing me, are you, old woman?"

"I am asking how I shall die in my sleep with you around. You will worry me to death first."

"Since when do you object to attention?"

She laughs, but it morphs into an ugly hacking that summons Miss Chiquita back upstairs. The dog leaps on the bed and howls at the ceiling, the way I want to, as she labors to catch her breath.

When the fit finally passes, I wipe pink froth of her lips. She's bitten her tongue. "You're too sassy for your own good," I say. I push black hair off her forehead. Strands come back with my fingers.

"Is everything okay up there?" Jones calls.

I tell him I'll be down in a second.

Irena motions towards the door. "Go on already. I need my beauty rest. My boy is coming in the morning, you know. I want to be energized and pink like that bunny with the batteries on TV."

Her boy. Jorge the Turd. In the morning he'll be here with the papers, the contract selling the Bit. Her land. This house. My home. She's going to sign them, and how the hell could I argue that she shouldn't. I bend and make her promise she'll stay in the bed until I get back. "You're going to break your neck on those steps."

"Oh, that I should be so lucky."

I wince. She strokes my hand. "You should be asleep yourself. Tomorrow is your big job interview. Are you nervous?"

"Not a bit. Who wouldn't want to hire Irena Little's right hand man?"

"You are full of shit. But they will like you anyway." Irena squeezes my fingers. "You will make April proud. Then, you marry her and be happy ever after like me and my Rut."

"You see that in your crystal ball or the tarot cards?"

"I see it here." She taps her heart.

I squeeze her hand. "You say this dog needs to pee?"

"She does. Bad. Her bladder's the size of a thimble. "

I laugh and call Chiquita to me.

"You keep your eyes on my baby. I don't want her drowning in the pool while you are charmed by young boobies," Irena says.

"These girls ain't exactly my first skinny dippers, you know."

"I know. You been around here forever. Too long, I think. I was still beautiful, like Elizabeth, when you come. Remember? You have a crush on me back then."

"Everybody had a crush on you is the way I've heard it. What is it Rut said? Liz Taylor wished she was as pretty as you?"

She giggles. "April is lucky. You are sweet, Deacon, a good man. Just a little crazy like my Rut." She looks at me, and I see the question coming. "Have you told her yet?"

I look away. "I will when the time is right." I scoop up Chiquita. "I got to get going before the dog pisses all over the bed, and Tom Jones calls the cops on our naked girls. I won't be gone long."

"Don't hurry. I be here."

I switch off the lights. "Sweet dreams."

I'm almost out the door when she speaks across the darkness. "My chinki, I know something about the power of words and I know everything about the meanness of people, much more than you, though you know enough. You carry the shame they give you all these years. When will you see that the shame is on them? Don't let the cruel ones take anything more from you. You tell this woman that I know you love everything. April will trust her heart, I promise you."

I hang my head. I'd give anything to believe her.

Wendy Oglesby has worked most of her professional life in entertainment marketing, but her avocations are writing, her pets, golf and the South Carolina Gamecocks. A graduate of the University of South Carolina College of Journalism, Wendy has published articles in newspapers and magazines and is a winner of two Charlotte Writer's Club contests, including the Elizabeth Simpson Smith Short Story Contest. She lives in Charlotte with her husband David, two dogs and a bunch of cats. When she's not marketing Broadway shows for Blumenthal Performing Arts or cheering on the Gamecocks, she is working on her first novel.

NONFICTION
First Place

The Red Dog

Wendy C. Oglesby

The red dog staggers into the road. A horn blasts. Tires squeal. I cringe. But the morning traffic pauses and he wobbles on.

Skeletal. Head down. Muzzle nearly scraping the asphalt. A chain, thick as my pinkie, dangles from his neck. It looks like something you'd use to stake out an elephant, and I am so startled by it, I almost miss the leg. A hind one dangles, shriveled and useless. He looks worse than dead.

I let out my breath. He's across at last, and the cars move again. He collapses under an oak and I drive past, chewing my lip and cursing my luck for being here at this moment. Why must this become my problem? I can name half-a-dozen good reasons not to get involved with this dog.

My husband and I are cat people. None of our six cats or my husband will be happy about a dog.

Our vet limits her practice to cats.

Our yard isn't fenced.

The damn dog is horribly injured and likely dangerous. Maybe rabid. I think about my mother and the shots she took after trying to rescue a stray kitten from under a school bus.

I'm not making all that much money, and this dog's medical bills will be a year of car payments.

I'm wearing my favorite green silk dress.

I turn around.

The dog ignores me as I walk up. "Hey dog." No reaction. He is past curious. Past growling. Past biting. I eye his ruined leg. It oozes black fluid and white maggots.

I focus on his head and the thick, heavy chain encircling his neck. My stomach knots. His coat is long, filthy and matted, but underneath the dullness is the promise of bronze. Some red hairs are tipped in black and other blonde.

He gazes at me. Dull-eyed and defeated. I make up my mind. "Come on." I tug on the chain. He stumbles to his feet and we walk slowly to the car.

He lacks the strength to climb inside. I grasp him around his middle and lift him into the front seat of my gold Accord. He truly is a bag of bones, tall as my knee, but barely heavier than our fattest cat. He settles on his gaunt haunches and stares straight ahead. You'll be all right, I tell him. "We'll get you something to eat."

I remember a vet office on South Tryon and head in that direction, chattering nonsense to the dog and wondering how much damage his rotten leg is doing to my beige velour. He listens, but makes no sound. I'm happy for his reservation because I suspect our relationship will be brief.

At the vet I tell the girl behind the desk I've found a dog, and I suspect he'll need a leg amputated. I hand her my credit card and she follows me back to my car. Her eyes widen. I tell her again this is not my dog. I assure her I would never allow an animal of mine to get into this kind of shape because I love animals, especially cats. I say I don't really want or need a dog, but feel sure my father or my sister will take him. They live out in the country. She listens and helps me get the dog out of the car. Inside, she runs my credit card and takes my phone number. "Good luck, red dog," I say as she takes him away.

I call my husband at work and tell him what I have done. "The cats won't like a dog," he says. I tell him I doubt the dog will live. I tell him if it does, I will get Daddy to take it. I tell him not to worry.

In the afternoon, the vet tech calls. They have cleaned the leg and given him morphine. He is a good dog, she says. Quiet and stoic. They removed the chain with a bolt cutter. The vet is still evaluating. It's an iffy situation. I relay this information to my husband. "Don't get your hopes up," I warn him.

He laughs.

The vet calls during dinner. The maggots are back. Since they cleaned the leg this afternoon, another brood has hatched. This is as bad as it sounds, a sign the infection is systemic and un-stoppable. The red dog's a goner. She advises me to put him down.

"Are you sure?" I say. She is.

I feel the hook sliding out of me. The vet tells me I did a compassionate thing to pick him up, that he was in terrible pain. Surgery, however, will cost thousands of dollars, and as there is so little hope of him surviving, the best thing to do is put him out of his misery.

The vet is kind. She wants me to feel okay about this, to give me absolution. I am grateful and guilty. After all, we didn't want a dog. After all, we are not rich. After all, we did all we could.

I tell her to put him to sleep.

My husband surprises me. He frowns across the table as I sit back down. "There's *nothing* they can do?" he asks. I don't know if he's disappointed in science or the red dog's fate. I tell him it was going to cost a fortune and the outcome was very poor.

He digests my words. "I hate dogs anyway," he says finally, and I know he is thinking of the German short-hair that killed Nicholas, our Siamese cat.

Not all dogs kill cats, I remind him. This one might have been all right.

The phone interrupts. The vet has a proposition. Would we pay for the dog's medications if she donated the surgery and he survived? For a moment, I am put out, annoyed that she has re-opened this can of worms. She explains she has never performed this particular amputation and could use the practice. She does not believe he will live regardless, but there is a sliver of a chance.

I cover the phone and ask my husband what he wants to do. He grimaces, wishing – I know – that I had taken another road to work to work this morning. Wishing he was not a party to this decision. Wishing, always wishing, that he had brought Nicholas inside that awful day when he ran out for groceries.

He shrugs. "Do whatever you think," he says.

I do what I feel.

Another autumn morning and my dog quivers beside me, antici-pating the moment I will open the door. I turn the knob and he hurtles past, racing for the fence line. Blackbirds scatter into a perfect cobalt sky. Beau prances in air crispy as mountain apples, delighted with himself. He is glossy red and handsome as dogs come. So fast and nimble that only the sharp-eyed spot it – the missing hind leg.

Some people see him a dozen times or more before they notice. But once they do, they gasp and ask. What happened? We say the vet believes he was used as bait by dog fighters. They freeze, shocked. Someone hurt this dog?

This dog? Who smiles all the time. Who adores everyone. Who sleeps with our cats curled between his forelegs. This dog. Who my husband grudgingly admits is "as good as they get." Someone hurt him with forethought and intent. I steam in the October chill, hot as the urine Beau splashes on the remains of the daylilies. Done, he lopes across the frost-tipped grass, tail high as a flag, while I ponder cruelty and meanness and the infinite human capacity for both.

The world is awash in missing limbs.

How do you keep that from changing you?

Beau likes to visit my father in the country. In town at our house, he is an only dog, but here, my father has a pack. Beau loves his own kind, and he lunges from the back seat into the middle of them all. Molly the Australian shepherd. Caroline, the Spitz-Golden mix that is my father's favorite. Curly, the black poodle-terrier. A new refugee, a brown hound with one blind blue eye. They howl and leap on one another.

My father laughs and says Beau is a lucky dog.

Out here, the land brims with squirrels and rabbits and room to run. The pack spies something in the field, and they take off after it, Beau in front. I shake my head. Their quarry is already up a pine. Another hopeless chase. But Beau runs on. All in. All optimist. All the time.

I try to take a lesson.

NONFICTION

Second Place

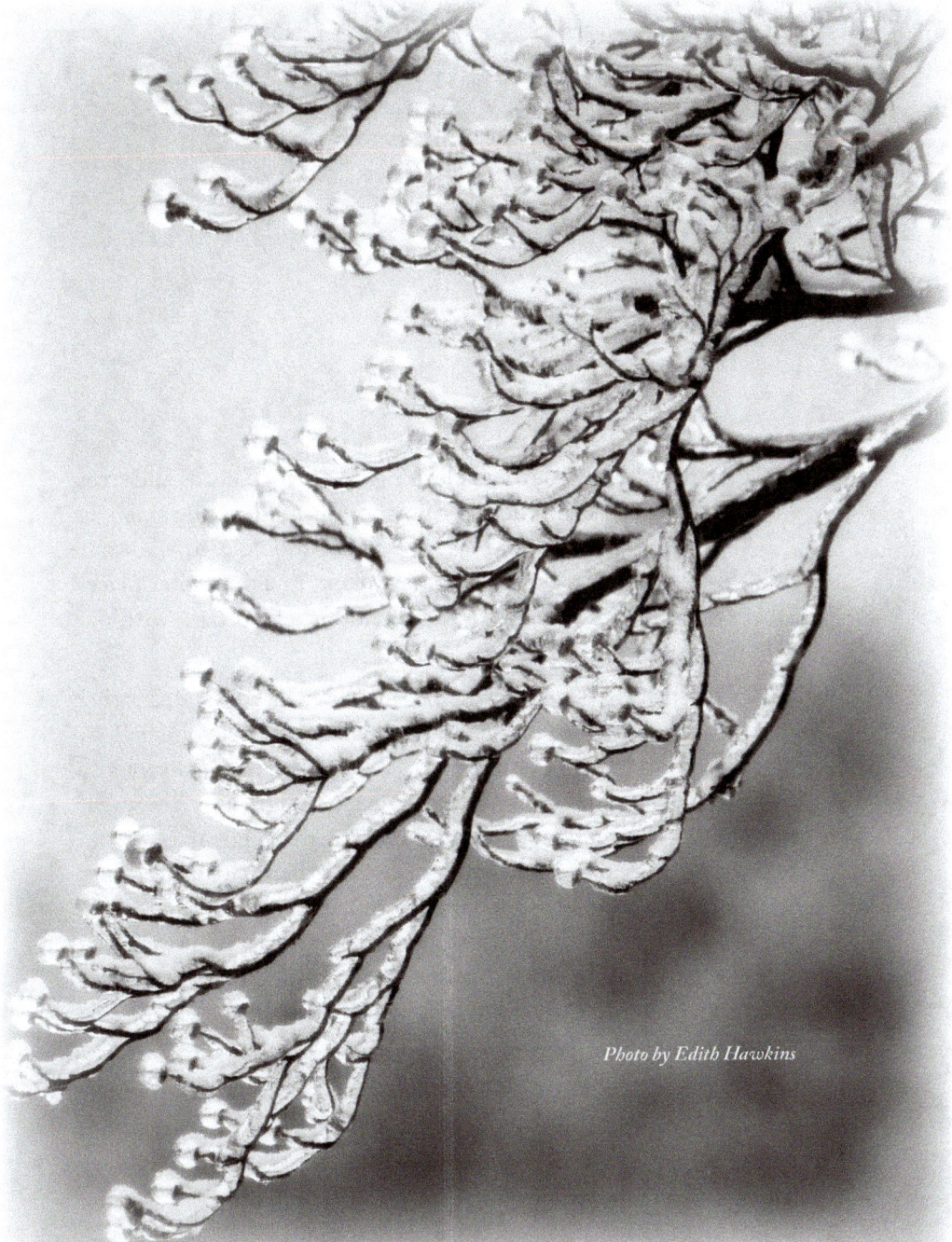

To Walk for a Shell

Michael Hugh Lythgoe

An Essay

Where I live we are still cleaning up downed limbs and trees from ice storm debris. Snow is appealing to the skiers in Vermont. It is cold again, but not too cold to walk outside this afternoon. To walk is to daydream; imagine other places, other walks, like the Manassas National Battlefield Park with our golden retriever.

Recently, I walked on the beach at Pawleys IsIand, another beach comber looking for shells. My prize was a scallop shell, inserted in a draft of a composition. One of my friends quoted a reference to a poem by Sir Walter Raleigh. "Pilgrimage": *Give me my scallop shell of quiet.* I was reminded of the pilgrimage associated with the scallop shell, the walk in northern Spain to honor the way of St. James. When our sons were born, we lived in Spain, but never made that walk. Now, our sons are grown, married, the eldest with three daughters. Some of the walks we took as they were growing up come back; other walks we never made, nor ever will make together.

For many years we lived in Virginia. My wife always liked driving west to Skyline Drive and hiking in the Shenandoah National Park, along the Blue Ridge Mountains. Our youngest son, Christopher, wanted to be carried. He got upset when we teased him to keep going, saying *you can make it*. Now we laugh about that hike. Earlier still we hiked in Indiana around the covered bridges in Brown County. Christopher rode on my shoulders. Later, we lived in England. Our sons attended British schools. We took two memorable hikes while living there.

At the time I was serving as an Air Force officer, and was invited to spend time on leave at a home in Scotland left by a family for the RAF to enjoy. The family had lost five sons who served in the RAF in WW II. It was a wonderful facility, kind of like Downton Abbey, which now may be used by the RAF Benevolent Fund to house elderly RAF veterans.

That week end in Scotland was a great experience for our family, meeting other service families, hunting frogs in a pond at night, enjoying great Scottish breakfasts and doing a nine mile trek around a lake in the highlands. We celebrated the challenge and the accomplishment, when we returned to Alastrian House for drinks and the evening meal. Somewhere we have pictures. No written record. No details in a diary. Regrets.

One other long walk stands out during our four year stay in the UK. We took the train down from London to Cornwall in the fall of 1980. We stayed in a little place called Mousehole, which later that year lost a lifesaving ship in a terrible storm. It was a disaster long remembered in that small coastal village. After looking at maps we decided to take a coastal path south to the next seaside village and hike back to our Bed & Breakfast on the paved road. We did that. My wife remembers our stop at a pub when we climbed down off the steep cliff, and the refreshing, strong ale she downed. The Cornishmen were not sure about the American hikers, or the thirsty American wife at the bar. She earned the fishermen's respect.

My wife can no longer stand for long periods, nor can she hike. Our walks now are mostly with travel shows on TV.

Last summer we met our oldest son and his family, wife and three daughters, in Wyoming. We stayed near the Elk Refuge in Jackson Hole and drove with our granddaughters to take them horseback riding, and on through the Grand Tetons to see Old Faithful. That was our last walk with the three girls. The year before we had met to walk on the rim of the Grand Canyon.

Not only is it hard for my wife to travel, but the granddaughters are at the age when they are increasingly less interested in spending time with grandparents. This is a story others of our age tell. So when I walk now, I think of what walks can mean, even if I did not appreciate them fully at the time.

Poets are known to be walkers. Think of John Keats hiking in Scotland, and Ireland. Wordsworth walking around his cottage in the Lake District. Wallace Stevens, insurance executive and poet, was famous for composing on his daily walks to his office. He always walked when he traveled on business to Florida or Tennessee. The popular British poet, Simon Armitage, proved the poet as walker and troubadour can still live off his poems from one end of the British Isles to the other. He walked the Pennine Way in the north, and in 2013 walked to Lands End. By all accounts, he was given shelter, food and drinks all along his route – for the price of his readings in pubs and art galleries along the way.

The late American poet, A.R. Ammons, who taught at Cornell, wrote: *a poem is a walk.*

Poems have beginnings and endings. We must breathe in and out as we walk and as we write. Writing is a physical action. Many writers travel with books of poems, Christopher Merrill, who heads the writing program at Iowa, visited war zones in the Balkans. He traveled with the Collected Poems of Saint-John Perse – poet-diplomat – who traveled across China before leaving France ahead of Nazis.

Poems are good company.

We began our walk reflecting on a scallop shell, a pilgrimage route in Spain. As I walk, my own pilgrimage to grave sites in Indiana along the Ohio River, where my parents are buried comes to mind, along with scenes of the Benedictine Monastery near my place of birth. Life is a long walk, a journey. Sometimes we pause, sometimes we push on, we miss some of the sights along the way.

It is good from time to time to write down what we see. To write where we walk, while we still can. Soon it will be Easter. During Lent the American Seminarians in Rome walk to the old, beautiful little-known small churches, the station churches. Walks can be a way to remember, a way to prayer. To find a shell on a walk is to find help on our way. A walk may add to or recover memories. Footsteps are like words on a page.

The pear trees appear in white mantillas for the season. They glow bright as if they know they are already fading into green at the tips. The Judas trees show Lenten purple. The forsythia bush has specks of gold, a Midas touch. It is the Ides of March. We know the road will come to a dead end. But for now spring makes the world seem to be an open road.

Walk on.

Photo by Stephen Nakatani
Flickr.com
Used under CC License

MICHAEL HUGH LYTHGOE is a Hoosier by birth. He studied at The University of Notre Dame and St. Louis university, served as a career officer in the USAF, and later earned an MFA from Bennington College. He has lived in Aiken with his wife, Louise, since 2004. Mike has taught at USCA for the Academy For Lifelong Learning, and served as President. One of his current obsessions is herons. His poetry collection, *Holy Week*, is available as an ebook. He has two nominations for a Pushcart. Recent work appears in *Windhover, Christianity and Literature, Bluestreak, Cairn, Spillway, SixFold, Pea River, Innisfree, The Poetry Society of SC Yearbook of winning poems 2014*, and *The Petigru Review*.

SHORT FICTION

Honorable Mentions

Legacy of the Ring

by Mary Edelson

The Ribbons

by Ferguson Williams

CARRIE McCRAY
MEMORIAL LITERARY
AWARDS

Photo by Michael Hugh Lythgoe

JUDGES

FIRST CHAPTER
OF A NOVEL

C. Hope Clark

C. HOPE CLARK is the author of four traditional mysteries, all through Bell Bridge Books: *Lowcountry Bribe* (2012), *Tidewater Murder* (2013), and *Palmetto Poison* (2014) in the Carolina Slade Mystery Series, and *Murder on Edisto* (2014) in the Edisto Island Mystery Series. She is also author of the frequently requested *The Shy Writer Reborn* (2013). Her books have won the Silver Falchion Award and the EPIC awards for ebooks. Hope is editor of FundsforWriters.com, a resource for writers that's won *Writer's Digest's* 101 Best Websites for Writers for the past 14 years. The FundsforWriters newsletter reaches forty thousand readers each week. Her articles have appeared in *Writer's Market* (Writer's Digest Books 2012, 2013), *Guide to Literary Agents* (Writer's Digest Books 2012, 2013), *Writer's Digest Magazine*, *The Writer Magazine* as well as numerous other trade publications. She's a frequent guest blogger for writing and business sites, and she often speaks across the country at conferences and book fair events as well as book stores across the Carolinas.

fundsforwriters.com
chopeclark.com

" Nobody understands the power of writing more than an author. Not only are the words powerful to readers, who all too often mistake good writing for easy work, but they are personally empowering for the creator. To spend precious years to perfect phrasing and then see work come to fruition in a contest, on a bookshelf, or on Amazon, is a satisfaction only another artistic creator can understand. Our words read, discussed, accepted, and honored give our lives meaning, infusing the world with our thoughts and beliefs long after our bodies are gone. A strong sense of eternity we all crave. "

Bruce Holsinger

BRUCE HOLSINGER, a fiction writer and award-winning literary scholar, is Professor of English at the University of Virginia, where he teaches courses on medieval and modern literature. His debut novel, *A Burnable Book* (William Morrow/HarperCollins), is set in the alleys and halls of medieval London, where the poets Geoffrey Chaucer and John Gower spent much of their lives. The sequel, *The Invention of Fire*, will appear in spring of 2015. *The Washington Post* has called Bruce "a graceful guide to the 14th century," while *The New York Times Book Review* hails his protagonist John Gower as "the perfect narrator and amateur sleuth," noting that the novel "delivers up a world where even the filth is colorful." Bruce's nonfiction books have won multiple awards from scholarly organizations, and his academic work has been supported by fellowships from the Guggenheim Foundation, the National Endowment for the Humanities, and the American Council of Learned Societies. He has appeared on NPR's *Here and Now* and *To the Best of Our Knowledge*, and lectures regularly on medieval culture and historical fiction to audiences around the world.

bruceholsinger.com

SHORT

FICTION

Maggie Schein

MAGGIE SCHEIN is the author of two books: *Lost Cantos of the Ouroboros Caves* (Hunt Press 2013) and *Lost Cantos of the Ouroboros Caves, Expanded Edition* (Story River Books 2014), Forward by Pat Conroy and Audiobook narrated by Grammy winner Janis Ian.

Maggie was born in Atlanta, GA, finished high school and college in NY and then moved to Chicago for graduate school, where she earned her doctorate from The University of Chicago's Committee on Social Thought. She currently works as a Research Director for the Institute for Advanced Study in Princeton. She lives in Beaufort, SC, where each day the incense from tea olive bushes, salted winds from the ocean, seasoned wafts from the marsh and the primal composting of soil raises her head in wonder. She lives with her motley menagerie 2 rescued pit bulls, 3 cats, the occasional drop–in owl, orphaned raccoon, or lost dog, and her beloved soul-mate and husband, Jonathan Hannah.

maggieschein.com

" Congratulations to every author who had the courage and the passion to share their stories. Keep telling them and listening to them! Thank you for the honor of trusting me to judge them. "

NONFICTION

Cynthia Boiter

CYNTHIA BOITER, founder and editor of *Jasper Magazine,* is the author of *Buttered Biscuits – Short Stories from the South* (2012), *Red Social* with artist Alejandro Garciá-Lemos (2013), editor of *A Sense of the Midlands* (2014) and *The Limelight – A Compendium of Contemporary Columbia Artists,* (2013), contributor to *Hub for the Holidays* (2013), *State of the Heart,* (2013), and *Inheritance* (2001). She is the 2014 winner of the Elizabeth O'Neill Verner Governor's Award for the Arts.

THE PETIGRU Competition REVIEW

FICTION

Photo by Jayne Bowers

John-E-Mail

Barbara V. Evers

To: John@freedommail.com
From: Sweetiepie321@girlmail.com
Date: February 15, 2006, 2:13:32 am
Subject: Happy Valentine's Day

Dear Johnny,

I misss you so much. I thought today would be awful! All of the girls getting flowers and candy and stuff. Depressed me! But then I thought about you defending our country. Boy did I feel guilty. I'm so selfish. : (

Did you get the card and candy, yet? I hope I sent them in time.

I felt so left out, today. I rented *Cold Mountain* because Nicole Kidman knows how I feel. You know how she writes her boyfriend and tells him to come home to her and he does? I wish you could do that. I was going to veg out and watch it all alone.

But, anyway, Trip and Julie made me go to some crazy party with them. I'm soooooo glad that they did cause I met a guy who just got back from Iraq. He made me feel so close to you. He told me stories and stuff that I know you can't. I wish it was you telling me these things. Come home to me.

Lots of love and hugs,

Ally

* * *

To: Sweetiepie321@girlmail.com
From: John@freedommail.com
Date: February 15, 2:12:54 am
Subject: Valentine

Hey baby! Happy Valentine's Day! I wanted to call you tonight, but I couldn't get through. We've had busy days. Lots happening. I thought about you today when we passed a girl by the side of the road. We thought she was just watching the trucks, but it got crazy and that's the last time I had time to think til now. I miss you. Wish I could have talked to you today.

Love ya! Johnny

* * *

To: John@freedommail.com
From: TheTrip@myemail.com
Date: February 15, 2006, 3:03:24 am
Subject: Sorry Dude

Hey!

Sorry guy my cell died. I had your ring and was going to give Ally the phone when you called. I failed you man. She was really down when we picked her up. I know she'll say yes. The party helped, though. She kept talking about you to some marine from Iraq.

* * *

To: TheTrip@myemail.com
From: John@freedommail.com
Date: February 15, 2006, 12:43:19 pm
Subject: Re: Sorry Dude

No problem about the phone. I'll work on another time to propose. They say I'll be home in June. Maybe I'll wait until then.

Who's the marine?

* * *

To: John@freedommail.com
From: Sweetiepie321@girlmail.com
Date: February 15, 2006, 7:16:43 pm
Subject: Miss You

Dear Johnny,

Did you notice that we were emailing each other at the same
time! Wow, we are so meant to be! I got your card. It would've
been better if you were here, though. I miss you so much. I saw
Glen, again. The marine. He keeps telling me about his adventures in Iraq. It sounds so dangerous. I had a nightmare about
you last night. You were in trouble and Glen saved you! Isn't that
funny? It felt so real. Please, please, please be careful.

Gotta go. Glen is taking me over to Julie's house. He makes me
feel so close to you.

Love ya!

* * *

To: TheTrip@myemail.com
From: John@freedommail.com
Date: February 16, 2006 9:16:44 am
Subject: Glen

Trip! Who's this Glen guy? What's going on?

* * *

To: John@freedommail.com
From: Sweetiepie321@girlmail.com
Date: February 17, 2006 2:23:21 am
Subject: I feel stupid

Dear Johnny,

You must think I'm a ditz! Glen told me that if you were emailing me at 2 am in Iraq that it's not 2 am here. I thought it was
SO romantic how we emailed each other at the same time and
I was just wrong. How stupid can I be? Please don't think I'm
dumb.

I miss you. Glen's stories make your world so real to me. Do you
know he was Special Ops? Isn't that exciting?

Ally

* * *

To: John@freedommail.com
From: TheTrip@myemail.com
Date: February 17, 2006, 6:14:14 pm
Subject: Re: Glen

Dude, Glen's bad news. I met Julie and Ally for lunch and he was there. All the girls love him. He's so full of it. He claims he captured Saddam. What crap! They're all eating it up, especially Ally. She keeps saying it makes her closer to you but man I think she's getting pretty close to old Glen > : {

Better watch out!

* * *

To: John@freedommail.com
From: MarineforLife@hero.com
Date: February 17, 2006 11:56:33 pm
Subject: Ally

John,

Hey man, you don't know me, but we're brothers. I got back from Iraq last month and I met Ally a few days ago. You're one lucky dude. I lost my girl while I was over there, so I'm gonna keep a close eye on Ally for you. Don't worry man. I got ya covered.

Glen

* * *

To: John@freedommail.com
From: Sweetiepie321@girlmail.com
Date: February 18, 2006 6:14:59 PM
Subject: You!

Hi Johnny!

You know how you always beg me to get out more? Well, I'm doing it! Glen is making sure of it. He says he's keeping the guys away for you. Isnt' that sweet? Did he email you? I gave him your address so he could encourage you too. He's done so much over there. He helps me so much. I don't miss you as much when he's around.

Ally

* * *

To: Sweetiepie321@girlmail.com
From: John@freedommail.com
Date: February 20, 2006, 11:47 pm
Subject: Re: You!

Dear Ally,

I love you. I miss you. I'm a little worried about this Glen guy. What unit is he from? Be careful baby? I can't wait to see you. I have a big surprise for you.

Love John

* * *

To: Sweetiepie321@girlmail.com
From: John@freedommail.com
Date: February 21, 2006, 11:21:26 pm
Subject: Checking In

Ally,

What's up? I've not heard from you in days. I miss you. I think about you all the time. They're sending us home in May, now. I know it keeps changing, but I can't wait to see you. I've got something big to talk to you about.

Love John

* * *

To: Sweetiepie321@girlmail.com
From: John@freedommail.com
Date: February 22, 2006, 10:17:43 am
Subject: Are you OK?

Hey baby, what's up? I miss you. I love you. Is your email not working? I miss getting your daily emails. Waiting for you.

John

* * *

To: John@freedommail.com
From: Sweetiepie321@girlmail.com
Date: February 23, 2006, 4:39:12 am
Subject: Re: Are you OK?

Dear John

Photo by Edith Hawkins

Phenomenon

Wilson Lanford

The best day in Margaret's life had been the day she met Steve in the Pittsburgh bus station. A scared seventeen-year-old running away from home, she sat clutching her brown suitcase and the ticket to San Jose California where she planned to look up her youngest aunt. Sewn inside her coat pocket was $80, all the money she had in the world. A man seated across from her kept glancing at her over his paper. She had little life experience but her crazy family had made her wary and untrusting. Finally a boy close to her age sat down in the seat next to her ignoring her while reading a magazine and she relaxed a little.

Sneaking sideways glances, she thought him quite handsome in his leather vest and white undershirt. The intoxicating smells of Aqua Velva and hormones came off him in waves. Males in her family became misshapen, almost monstrous, as hormones seized their bodies pushing their faces into angles changing their voices, and coating them in hair. Eventually they melted into adult forms leaving behind the coarse adolescent bodies. But this boy, who was old enough to shave but still not yet a man, had something angelic in his features, a softness of look, a pinkness of cheek, and his hands were tapered, not rough.

When he offered her a stick of gum, she was giddy with delight. He told her he was returning from Fort Monmouth, New Jersey, where he had visited his cousin in the army and now was waiting for the bus to take him home to Nebraska. It turned out, they were traveling on the same bus.

They spent the next two days in conversation, and he outlined his big plans for the future. She hung on every word, seduced by his optimism. He seemed genuinely interested in her, and, as they warmed to each other, a relationship developed. He had charmed her into getting off the bus before California saying how special she was, promising to take care of her.

Even now, Steve still raved about her being the woman he loved, but it seemed routine. His attention was drawn elsewhere as soon as the words were out of his mouth.

The best day of her life had been followed by five years of dull gray days and discouraging circumstances as they settled in a routine living with his mother. Free rent meant waiting on Ma's every need.

At first Margaret was glad to be part of someone's family, but what she really wanted was her own family, her own house. Steve put off the idea of a baby, saying they couldn't afford it. As time went on, Margaret realized a baby would only keep her in this situation with no hope for a future without Ma, who was always hungry and always complaining.

The change in Margaret's life started out as a routine Saturday. That morning Margaret decided to make pancakes in the oiled cast iron pan. Dancing droplets of water signaled the perfect temperature for pouring pancake batter. When the edges of the batter bubbled she turned them with the oversized spatula. As the pancake landed cooked side up, Margaret was startled to see a face looking back at her.

She inhaled and muttered, "Mother of God."

Steve wandered into the kitchen yawning and scratching his belly. "What'd you say? That smells good. What are you making?" He wandered over to put his arms around her. Margaret quickly scooped the pancake onto a plate, and Steve reached for it.

"No," Margaret screamed, "not that one." Then calmer, "It's ruined, I'll make you another." She put the plate in the oven and poured more batter into the pan.

Steve sat at the kitchen table, and she handed him a cup of coffee. She turned the pancake over with trepidation. "Jesus," she muttered.

"Hey, what's gotten into you?" Steve said.

"Nothing," Margaret whispered. Another plate joined the first in the oven.

"When are those pancakes gonna be ready?"

"I'm not sure, I can't seem to get them to turn out right this morning."

"Well fry an egg or something, I'm starving. And Ma's like a bear with a sore toe when she's hungry."

One more try, thought Margaret. This could not be happening. It must be her imagination.

Again she poured batter into the waiting pan and watched for the tiny bubbles to form. This time she didn't have to wait to turn it over. The batter ran and formed a picture along with the bubbles on top of the pancake. Did she dare flip it? Instead, she pushed the pan off the burner and covered it with a lid. She cracked eggs and stirred them in another pan.

Ma's heavy footsteps sounded on the wooden stairs, each downward step accompanied by a grunt of effort. She made her way to the kitchen.

"Where's breakfast?" Ma said.

"It's coming," said Steve. "Margie started pancakes but screwed them up."

"Where are they? I don't mind screwed up pancakes." Ma lurched toward the stove and lifted the lid off the pan. "What is it? It looks like an animal." She squinted at the pancake. "You didn't turn it over. What's the matter with you Margie?" She sat heavily at the kitchen table. "Where's my coffee?"

Margaret plated the eggs, jammed bread into the toaster and poured a cup of coffee. She set the eggs and coffee down in front of Ma.

"Where's the toast? Eggs aren't any good without toast," Ma said.

"It's coming." Margaret grabbed another plate for Steve's eggs.

"Honest to God, Steve," Ma carped, "I don't know what you saw in her. She's useless."

Steve read the newspaper as Margaret set the toast in front of Ma then returned to the stove for Steve's eggs.

"I'm still hungry." Ma said. "Where are those ruined pancakes? Are they edible?"

"Yes," Margaret said, "but you can't have them."

"What did you say? Steve, did you hear her? Are you going to let her get away with that?"

Steve slowly rose from the table and came over to where Margaret was staring at the pan. In a low voice he said, "What's going on, Margie? You know Ma gets what she wants."

"Not this time," Margaret said in a fierce whisper. She pulled the plates from the oven. "Look at the first pancake I made this morning. What does it look like?"

"I dunno, is it a face?"

"Yes, it's a face. It's the face of the Madonna."

"You mean the rock star?"

"No, Steve. The Madonna, the Holy Mother."

Surprise flashed across Steve's face. "But we're not Catholic."

"Neither was she. And surely you recognize this one. It's Jesus, not a rock star either."

"What's going on over there?" Ma said.

"Show her," Steve said. "Ma, you're not going to believe this."

Margaret set down the plates in front of the woman.

Ma glared at Margaret. "So? Where's the syrup?"

Ma picked up her fork. Steve pulled the plates back.

"Look again, Ma. This is Jesus and this is Mary."

"Very funny. Where's Joseph?" She reached for the plates, but Steve moved them out of her reach.

"Oh no, you don't. This is our big chance. A grilled cheese sandwich with the face of Jesus sold on eBay for $28,000. Your appetite will have to wait." Ma glanced from one to the other in disbelief.

Margaret took over. "We have to make sure nothing happens to ruin them until we decide what to do next. And don't tell anyone or we'll have the whole town standing in our front yard."

"For once she's right, Steve," Ma said. "No need to tell all your pool hall buddies." It was like a benediction, and Margaret let out a sigh of relief.

Later, when the house was quiet with Ma "resting her eyes" in the living room and Steve off to hang out with his friends, Margaret took the lid off the pan and stared down at the shape. It had solidified into a face with horns and a pointed chin. Bubble outlined eyes stared at her. Was this the devil mocking her? She put the lid back on to the pan and shoved it to the back burner.

She wrapped the other two pancakes in foil, stacked them

on a plate and thought about what to do next. God was telling her something. She just had to figure out what.

Church wasn't a regular part of Margaret's life, though she had always felt the Almighty was her friend and had something special in store for her. In her desperation she had prayed for something, anything, even a disaster, to give her a chance to test herself, to triumph over life. Now something new and unexpected had happened, and she had to know what it meant before it was snatched away. Listening once more to the silence of the house, she put on her coat, picked up the two pancakes and headed out the door.

"Scared" Heart Church, as Steve called it, was on Main and Aberdeen. She must be sure not to slip up and say that. The sign read church was open for confession on Saturday with no Mass scheduled. Father McMahon was listed as the priest. She entered the heavy wooden door and looked around at the faithful few praying in the pews. There was a bang as the heavy door of the confessional swung shut behind a departing parishioner. Margaret waited, looking around for someone to guide her. Perhaps the priest was in the box, so she tiptoed to the door and opened it to find a squat man in black sitting inside.

"You're supposed to go in the other side to confess," he said. "But you're not Catholic are you?"

"No, I'm not, and I don't want to confess, I want to show you something."

"Well you'll have to wait. Confession is from 2:00 pm to 4:00 pm."

"Do you have many people who come to confess?"

"No, but it's a good time to take a nap. What did you want to show me?"

"I was making pancakes this morning, and they have pictures of Jesus and Mary on them."

The priest sighed. "Come with me, my dear."

He rose and shut the heavy door behind him leaving the "In Use" sign on the door. He showed Margaret into his office and settled behind his desk in a squeaky leather chair. "Let's see what you've got."

Margaret carefully unwrapped the foil package and shoved the plate toward him. He paused before speaking.

"Well, I see two faces I know very well. People often see them in tree trunks, cracks in the wall, or in the clouds. There is a name for this phenomenon, apophenia, the tendency to see human faces in inanimate objects. Do you see things like this often?"

Margaret hesitated, feeling the miracle slip away from her. "No. This is the first time it's happened. Maybe because I've been praying for something unusual to happen."

"Well, my dear, you are not the only one praying for something out of the ordinary. This church is on the brink of being closed due to shrinking membership. A miracle would be just the thing to revive interest. But," and here he held up a cautioning hand, "I am not in the position to declare something a miracle. The Vatican has strict rules about that. Do you think it is a miracle?"

"I-I don't know," Margaret stammered. "That's why I came to see you. I thought you would know."

His next words to her were carefully phrased. "Obviously, something very special has occurred, as it is rare for two such images to occur in succession. What do you want to happen now? I see you are married. What does your family want to do?"

"Steve, my husband, wants to sell them on eBay, and his ma wants to eat them."

The priest laughed and Margaret did too in spite of herself. She knew when she got home the front yard would be full of Steve's friends wanting to see what he couldn't help but tell about.

Once it went public she would lose control. She wanted be the one to break the story, to hold onto the miracle and become identified with it. The town newspaper was a weekly so by the time the paper came out on Wednesday, it wouldn't be news. The television station's news featured hog futures or soybean prices and the weather.

"Do you think the TV station would cover this story?" she said. "Maybe they could interview me in front of the church – but you don't have to say anything. I don't want to get you in trouble with the Pope."

Father MacMahon's response was instantaneous. "I'll dial the number for you. Tell them you have pancakes which appear to be of a religious nature. Say no more, no less." He handed the phone to Margaret. "The public will make their own assumptions."

To Margaret's surprise the television station promised to send a crew to the church within the hour. While waiting, she and Father MacMahon practiced some Q and A, so by the time the TV crew arrived, she was no longer nervous.

Their questions just made her feel important. Inside she felt a real person growing she had all but forgotten.

"You are going to be on the 5:00 o'clock news, little lady," the news anchor joked. "Get ready to be famous."

When she returned home, she was not surprised to see the front yard full of Steve's friends surrounding him. He met her halfway up the sidewalk. "Where have you been? Ma missed lunch, and I'm afraid to go in the house. She'll be screaming about being neglected. You go get her calmed down."

At first, Margaret thought Ma was asleep in front of the TV but then she saw her lips were blue and she was not breathing. In her hand was a fork. On the TV tray was the partially eaten devil pancake. She must have choked on it. Margaret could imagine her calling for help and not being heard by Steve and his friends.

"That's right folks," the TV announcer said, "we have a genuine miracle right here in our little town. As we told you earlier, Margaret Jones found the faces of Jesus and Mary in pancakes this morning. In case you missed it at the top of the broadcast, here it is again."

Margaret saw her face in closeup on the TV and thought, who is that girl? She went upstairs and brushed her hair and put on some lipstick. Then she came downstairs and opened the front door.

"Steve," she yelled. "Your mother needs you."

The unusual Margaret had prayed for had happened. Her life would never be the same.

Gargoyle by Scott Wylie, Flickr
Used under CC License

Golfing Buddies

Richard Lutman

Harry Stevens stood in his silk pajamas on the back lawn of his house with a titanium driver in his hands and a bucket of golf balls at his feet. He bent down, took a ball from the bucket, teed it up, stepped back, tried a few practice swings, then lined up his feet with the ball. The club head struck just behind the label. He lifted his head in time to see the ball disappear into the darkness. It rattled off the pines that grew behind the house. He teed up another and hit it, then another and another until the balls sounded like gun fire as they ricocheted off the trees. His wife Sylvia watched him from the open bedroom window.

"You're an ass, Harry," she said loudly into the night. "A real fucking ass."

"They're findable," he said in his best golfer's voice, trying to ignore her. "They're findable." Under his breath he mumbled, "Bitch."

He took a final swing, heard the last of the golf balls hit the trees, put the club back in the bag and brought it inside. He climbed the stairs to their bedroom. He stood in the dark of their room breathing heavily.

"That was pretty good," he said. "I finally got my drives straightened out. I really did."

"Wonderful," she said. "I got you those golf balls for your birthday. I didn't expect you to use them like that. Golf balls were what you asked for. You can be a real shit at times."

"In the morning I'll take the kids with me and we'll find the balls. We'll pretend we're looking for Easter eggs. As I was sitting downstairs with my drink I started thinking what it would be like to hit the balls into the woods, that's all. It was something I wanted to do."

"You're an ass," she said.

"You already said that."

"Well you are," she said.

"And you're a bitch."

"What did you expect after being married to you all these years?"

"I don't know," he said. "How about a nightcap? A good martini will fix everything up."

"I don't need to be fixed up," she said. "Didn't you hear me? I just want to get some sleep. I'm tired."

"You're always tired."

"How do you expect me to be?"

He shrugged, strode downstairs and clattered about the kitchen.

She stood at the head of the stairs. "You'll wake the children with all that noise."

"Good," he said.

He sat on the sofa and stared out into the night. She came downstairs and stood behind him.

"You're an asshole," she said.

"So what? There's lots of assholes in this world."

"But you're the biggest."

"At least I'm good at something," he said.

She laughed.

"I was thinking about our wedding party," he said into the dark. "Dancing under the tent all night long with the smell of freshly cut clover coming from the fields. I thought you were the most beautiful woman I'd ever seen."

Her strong, slender hands and the way her lips parted as she kissed him. He was seized with a spasm of yearning so sudden and so intense it left him quite dizzy with excitement and pleasure.

"I thought you wanted to go to bed," he said.

"I changed my mind."

"Just like you." he said.

"Fuck you."

"How about that martini?"

"I told you no," she said.

"Peanuts?" he said offering her the bowl.

She shoved the bowl at him, spilling peanuts onto the rug.

"What the fuck did you do that for?" he said.

"I wanted to."

"You're acting strange."

"How do you want me to act?" she said.

"I don't know."

He rose and opened the patio doors. The night was warm and very still. The sky was a mosaic of stars.

"You remember the time we went to the Village to see that sax player?" he said. "His solo started out soft and breathy with his head bent so low that you could hardly see the player's face. Then he lifted it up, and with his eyes closed the sound became so hard and clear and yearning that you would have thought he was playing a violin instead of a sax. This martini isn't too bad. Sure you don't want one?"

He turned away from the doors and started for the kitchen not looking at her as he passed.

"If I have one, then what?" she said.

"We'll talk."

"About what?" she said.

"Anything," he said. "Like we used to."

"I don't feel like it tonight."

"You don't feel like a lot of things tonight, do you?" he said.

"What do you mean by that?"

"I've made a whole pitcher of the stuff," he said. "I can't drink it all."

"Try," she said.

"Maybe I will."

"Don't be childish," she said.

"Fuck you." He lifted the pitcher from the kitchen counter to his lips and drank.

"All right," she said. "All fucking right."

He poured out a glass for her and dumped in an olive.

"Cheers," he said and watched her sip the drink. "That's better. What's the matter?"

"I'm getting fat," she said.

"Join Weight Watchers," he said.

"Maybe I'll start jogging," she said.

"Jogging."

"What's wrong with that?"

"I don't want you to, that's all," he said. "I've seen the way men look at women joggers."

"You look at them the same way," she said.

"That's not very funny."

"It wasn't meant to be, you prick."

The smell of recently cut grass came to him and wafted through the house. A car glided by, headlights threading through the thick summer heat.

"Remember our honeymoon and how it rained," she said. "The heater kept going out. We had to stay in bed the whole time. Lord it was fucking cold. It wasn't at all like I thought a honeymoon would be."

"And the motel restaurant ran out of food," he said. "We couldn't even get a cup of coffee."

"Yes," she said. "And when we first started going together, how we'd drive up to Connecticut and take long walks."

"You can't forget things like that," he said.

"I never thought I was making the wrong decision when I married you."

"What are you talking about?" he said.

"People do all sorts of odd things and they never know why," she said. "I can't explain it."

"You want a divorce?" he said.

"Let's go find the golf balls."

"Now?"

"Yes," she said. "Right now."

"I thought we were going to talk."

"Fuck the talk," she said.

He followed her out into the dark.

"Be careful you don't fall," he said.

"As if you care."

She stepped into the woods. A shriek from the shadows brought him running.

"Are you all right?"

She lay on the ground looking up at the sky, her nightgown around her shoulders.

"I'm fine. And I found a golf ball."

She was about to hand it to him, and then stopped, sliding her hand down over her taut belly, till she reached her pubis where she released the ball into her wiry hair.

"Where is it?" he said.

"You'll have to find it," she said.

Photo by Michael Hugh Lythgoe

Casket Fresh

Jodie Cain Smith

News of the death spread quickly throughout Huet's Point. It moved in whispers across porches and through open parlor windows. Near dusk, it escaped prim lips and landed in Ellie Weever's ear as she walked home from Hodges General Store.

The next morning, Ellie rose early, before dawn, and dressed by lamplight, eager to welcome her guests. With every button of her bodice secured and her apron tied around her slight waist, she carried the lamp from her bedroom, down the stairs, and through the kitchen.

She listened to the ticking of the parlor clock, floating past the furniture and sparse décor of her home. The ticking crept around darkened doorways and over the wooden floor. The sound seemed to grow louder against the silence of the house. Troubled by the ticking, Ellie walked to the pantry. She was filling her pockets with peppermints when she heard the banging on the death door.

With her pale fingers, Ellie slipped a peppermint into her mouth. She tied a handkerchief around her head just below her eyes. The soft, lace edges tickled her chin as she unlocked and pulled the death door, located off the parlor, open. She sucked on the peppermint while a white man and a sturdy Creole woman carried the casket through the door and set it on the table in the center of the parlor.

For nearly an hour, the man leaned against the parlor wall as Ellie and the Creole woman bathed and dressed the corpse. Already grey with death, the body was filthy. Not just with the evidence of the violent end, but with evidence of how he lived. With a wet rag, Ellie wiped the corpse's chest, arms, abdomen, feet, and legs.

"No need for 'im to look perfect," the man leaning against the parlor wall said as Ellie wiped her rag gently across a thigh. "He weren't all that clean when he's alive."

Ellie ignored the comment. She took great care in readying men for burial, even more than the women she had prepared over the last two years. From the moment the death door rattled, Ellie viewed any man in Huet's Point as her own, if only for the short time he lay in her parlor until the widow or mother or daughter appeared to take her man away.

After several more minutes, the corpse was dressed in a white linen shirt, black trousers, waistcoat, overcoat, and cravat. Although Ellie felt the cravat was a bit fussy for this particular guest, she always abided by the family's wishes. She bent over the casket to fold the corpse's arms over his chest. Her hand tingled when she felt rough calluses rub against her skin.

"You can go now," Ellie said through her kerchief. "I'll finish the preparations."

"Suit yourself," the man standing in her parlor said. "Guess you'll be needin' these." He reached his own filthy hand toward her and dropped three coins into her hand. "Let's go, Sabine."

Ellie placed the coins in her pocket and locked the death door behind the two visitors. In the kitchen, she scrubbed her hands at the porcelain basin and then rubbed a lavender salve deep into her skin. She retrieved another peppermint from her pocket and sucked air through her nose as the candy melted against her tongue.

With two additional lamps, she returned to the parlor. The sun peeked through the crease of the drawn curtains, but she dared not open them. Ellie couldn't stand the onlookers that gathered on the street in front of her house whenever she worked. And with the rate at which the people of Huet's Point lined up for their final journey, she could afford all the oil she could burn.

Ellie hoisted the heavy pine lid propped against the table and dragged it into the kitchen. She wouldn't need it again until after the viewing and felt it cluttered the space around her guest. As she pulled it over the lip of the kitchen floor, the wood slipped from her hand and smacked against the floor. She felt a jolt through her entire body as the sound echoed off the high ceilings, hard floors, and uninhabited rooms. The sting of a splinter pulsed in her finger as she walked back into the parlor and sucked harder on the peppermint.

"Well, Ray Don," Ellie said, smiling into the pine box, "let's see what I can do."

Ray Don Lawry, brigand of Huet's Point, may have been fresh in the casket, but he definitely didn't look casket fresh. His front was as horrific as the rear view. The bullet entered his left eye, split his skull, and exited out the back of his head. Considering the extent of Ray Don's wound, Ellie thought a simple burial would be best, but Widow Lawry had insisted on a viewing.

"Your lid got me good, Ray Don." Ellie dug her thumbnail into her finger near the splinter and winced as the wooden fleck emerged from beneath her skin. She stuck her finger in her mouth and sucked on the wound for a second. "That was a bad 'ol splinter," she told him. "But I forgive you. I know you didn't mean to hurt me."

Ellie picked up the silver comb from her table of supplies and ran the comb through Ray Don's hair, as if painting gentle strokes on a linen canvas.

"I really should thank you, I guess," Ellie said. "Even though it seems awful to thank a man for dyin'. But the Good Lord provides, Ray Don. Yes, He does. Even if all He's provided me with lately are ne'er-do-wells." Ellie paused and then said with conviction, "Yes, the Lord provides. He brought you to me, and for that, I give thanks."

Ellie attempted to stretch the dull grey strands of hair over as much of Ray Don's last moments as possible. After a few minutes, knowing the old man didn't have enough hair left to cover the entire wound, she gave up and placed the comb back on the table. She turned back to the casket and caressed Ray Don's good cheek with the back of her fingers. A charge surged through her body as she wondered what his skin felt like before the cold of death.

"You were strong once, weren't you, Ray Don? But tender, too. I bet you could be right tender."

She leaned over the coffin. Little ripples formed on the bridge of her nose beneath the kerchief as she examined the fatal wound. Shaking her head, she told Ray Don, "I just don't think Widow Lawry should have to see that hole in your face." Then Ellie whispered near his ear, "Of course, if'n you ask me, *Widow* Lawry shouldn't'a took on that name. And before you was dead. That's just bad juju."

She pulled another peppermint from her pocket, licked it, and then pulled it into her mouth with her tongue.

"A woman ought to be more grateful for a man in her life,

'specially a big, strong man like you." She tilted her head to the side and stared at the wound for several moments, and then, "Oh, I know just what you need!"

Up the stairs in her father's former bedroom, Ellie opened the trunk at the foot of the bed, dressed with a lace-trimmed quilt and linens since her father's death. She sifted through various mementos until she found his collection of eye patches, amassed over a lifetime of caring for the deceased, and chose a plain, black leather patch.

Back in the parlor, she opened her tub of greasepaint. Using an ochre-stained rag she blotted Ray Don's skin with her home-made concoction of lard, cornstarch, and clay until, after several minutes, his complexion didn't look quite so haggard.

"It's a shame to waste good beets on you, Ray Don," Ellie teased as she smashed two fresh beets in a wooden bowl. "But, everyone should look their best to meet their maker. I'm just not sure who exactly made you." She dipped one finger into the red beet juice and dabbed Ray Don's cheeks. "Yes, with the devil runnin' through your veins, I wonder if you'd be tender at all. Maybe not," she said and felt the lace of her kerchief tickle her chin again below her playful grin. "Oh, Ray Don, you do tease, don't you?"

The patch was the finishing touch. Gently, so to avoid the hole in the back of his skull, Ellie lifted the old man's head.

"I guess only the Lord knows who killed you, huh? Everybody's talkin' 'bout you and how good the shot was, but nobody's saying who did you in."

Ray Don's face grazed her bosom as she wrapped the strap around his head just above his ears, and positioned the patch over his left eye. For the third time that morning, her body prickled with longing.

"It's just a cryin' shame to come to such a vicious end, Ray Don. Just a cryin' shame."

Ellie shook her head and then straightened Ray Don's shirt collar. She retrieved the three pennies from her pocket and balanced one coin on Ray Don's lips and one on his right eye. After a moment of contemplation while rubbing the third coin between two fingers, she closed her hand around it. "I guess you cain't see outta that left eye no ways. You don't mind, do you, dearest?"

Content with Ray Don's appearance, she glanced at the clock centered on the mantle. Ray Don's final preparations ate up most of the time Ellie had hoped to use preparing herself for the viewing. In a rush, she tossed her combs, greasepaint, bowls, brushes, and rags in the leather satchel on the floor near the table and picked up the bowl of smashed beets. Then she blew out the lamps and went to the kitchen where she scrubbed her hands clean a second time. Back in the parlor, she pulled the curtains open. Sunlight flooded the room and cast a warm glow on Ray Don's face.

"God bless you, Ray Don," Ellie said, as she wrapped her fingers around the stiff handle of her leather satchel and admired her latest creation. "And if He cain't do that, maybe He'll have mercy on your soul."

In her bedroom, she placed the penny from her pocket on her vanity, set the satchel on the floor just inside the door, and quickly undressed. Her frock and apron she threw into a heap on the floor and then slipped into her favorite funeral attire: long, black silk with a fitted waist and high lace collar over several starched petticoats. She glided around her bedroom for a moment and listened to the swish of the layers. She glanced at her reflection in the bubbled mirror, stopped and pinched her cheeks. Maybe today, she thought to herself. Viewings for notorious no-gooders like Ray Don Lawry attracted every farmer, merchant, and fisherman across the bayou. Maybe today.

As long as the people of Huet's Point kept her in business she didn't need a husband, at least not financially, but she still held out hope that one day she wouldn't have to suck on peppermint or spread lye from the kitchen to the parlor and up the stairs or dig splinters from pine boxes out of her fingers or scrub her hands raw four times a day or listen to the silence of the house. She could leave the curtains open and move the china hutch from the dining room to the parlor and block the death door forever, and really know what a man, his warm skin, callused hands and broad shoulders would feel like.

"Ellie Dawson," Widow Lawry yelled from downstairs. "Get your rear end down here, now."

Startled, Ellie grabbed the penny from her dresser and stashed it in the hidden pocket of her full skirt.

"Widow Lawry," Ellie called from the landing, "is there a problem?"

"What the hell is on his face?" Widow Lawry asked, pointing one sausage-like finger inches from Ray Don's nose as Ellie rushed into the parlor.

"An eye patch, ma'am. I thought it best to cover the wound."

"Well, you thought wrong." Then Widow Lawry snatched the coins off his eyes and lips. "And he won't be needin' these where he's goin'." She extended her hand, palm up, to Ellie. "I know my idiot boy gave you three when he dropped off the old buzzard. Where's the third?"

Ellie took the third coin from her pocket and gave it to the widow. Embarrassed, she avoided Widow Lawry's gaze.

"Now you fix him right!" Widow Lawry shoved the coins into the crease between the two ample breasts threatening to escape her bodice.

"Ma'am?" Ellie asked the widow, taken aback by her harsh tone and offensive attire.

Widow Lawry pointed again at the eye patch. "You take that thing off him right now."

Ellie leaned over Ray Don and carefully removed the patch as Widow Lawry bent over the coffin, so close to Ellie that the widow's skirt brushed against her own. The dowager's hot, foul breath, like sulfur gas rising from the swamp, coated Ellie's neck in noxious fumes. She hoped the smell wouldn't linger in her hair as she slipped one hand into her pocket, digging for a third peppermint. Her pocket was empty so she held her breath as she removed the eye patch from Ray Don's face.

"That's better," whispered Widow Lawry, and then with pride, "now everyone can see the shot that finally put the bastard down."

Ellie looked into Widow Lawry's eyes and was surprised by the absence of grief.

"You're a smart girl, Ellie Weever, not to marry. Husbands only bring you trouble."

"Yes, ma'am," Ellie told the widow. "If you'll excuse me, I need a moment." Ellie nodded quickly and then walked back up the stairs, aching to be away from the widow.

Alone in her bedroom, she grabbed a peppermint from the pocket of her skirt heaped on the floor. She thought of Widow Lawry's dark eyes as she examined the candy and removed a fleck of lint from it.

"She's wrong," Ellie whispered.

She popped the peppermint into her mouth and bit down, grinding her teeth into the sugar. Maybe today, she thought again. Maybe today.

Lasting Impressions

Bob Strother

Clay Mason tipped the cardboard box, and an avalanche of glossy photographs slid out, consuming most of the dining room table. He shuffled them around, widening the pile, his eyes roaming left to right, up and down. He found one he liked and brought it close enough to see without his eyeglasses. In it, Clay sat at the helm of a ski boat – one nicely muscled arm gripping the steering wheel, his dark hair tousled, driven by the wind, aviator sunglasses shading his eyes. He felt the familiar pang of poignancy that often occurs when one is reminded of the passage of time – 40 years, in this case.

Movement caught his attention, and he glanced up to find his wife leaning on the doorjamb separating the dining room from the kitchen.

"Reveling in the glory days of your youth?" Betsy said. "And what on earth have you done to my table?"

"I am in the midst of a project, if you must know. And no, I'm not reveling. I'm merely selecting some appropriate photographs for my funeral montage."

Betsy gave him that look she used when she thought he'd

done or said something incredulous. Clay didn't much care for it – especially when he'd actually done or said something incredulous.

"You're joking, right?" she said. "You just had your annual physical. The doctor said you were in great shape. Why are you thinking about a funeral montage?"

"What the doctor said was 'you're in great shape for 70 years old.' In reality, I could sign off at any moment – heart attack, aneurism, stroke – who knows? Anyway, when I do go, I want people to remember that I was young once, not just some doddering old – "

"Fool?" Betsy offered. "Good luck with that. And by the way, with my luck, you'll probably live another thirty years." This time she slipped him that same mischievous grin she'd worn the day they first met. The one he couldn't keep himself from returning.

"Sarcasm does not become you, Betsy."

She pushed off the doorframe and said, "A healthy dose of sarcasm makes life with you a little more bearable."

With the smile still on his face, Clay watched as she returned to the kitchen. She still had the lithe body of a woman half her years – the sass, too, he thought – something he was short on the past few years. His gaze fell again to the array of photos scattered across the table. Some were from earlier, before he and Betsy were married, but most archived their life together. Not that Clay needed them to remember. The details were there, in his head, like some carefully packed footlocker that had withstood the constant inspection of time.

Saucy-tongued or not, Betsy had always been the one. When he'd fallen in love with her, he'd really had no choice. His heart had jumped into her and there it stayed. Odds were Clay would go before she did, and he sometimes hoped – selfishly, he knew – that would be the way it happened. He moved the photos around again using his forefinger to unearth ones nearer the bottom of the mass.

This one's a keeper, he thought, spying a shot of himself in ski garb perched on the side of a snow-white mountain. Beech Mountain, he figured, or maybe Sugar. It was hard to know – he'd skied every resort in North Carolina in those days. And there was one with his son, aged about twelve at the time, both of them shirtless, straddling a Yamaha dirt bike. Clay had only ridden the bike a couple of times, but fortunately, the photo had captured his roguish expression for all time.

Half an hour later, he'd selected a stack of two dozen photographs. His favorite, he reckoned, was one of him being pulled behind a ski boat, one hand on the rope handle, the other brandishing a half-empty bottle of Boone's Farm Strawberry Hill wine. The photos ranged from the time he was about ten years old until he was in his mid-fifties – before his hair started going gray and his throat began showing signs of a wattle.

Clay neatened up the stack and slid it into a six-by-nine manila envelope. He grabbed his coat from the hall closet and walked back into the kitchen. Betsy was there, at the stove, stirring a pot of fudge.

"I'm going down to Walgreen's," Clay said. "If the photos are already on a DVD, it'll be easier for the funeral home people to set up the montage."

"Are you serious?" Betsy asked.

He nodded. "Yes, I am."

She balanced the wooden spoon on the rim of the pot. "You do realize it's already starting to get dark, and you don't see so well at night, you know. Not to mention it's raining cats and dogs. Why don't you at least wait until tomorrow morning?"

Clay raised his hands, grasping the envelope of photographs like a TV evangelist might hold a Bible. "We aren't promised tomorrow, my dear."

Betsy retrieved the spoon and licked a bit of fudge from its edge. The glow from the oven light bathed her smooth face in a soft honey-colored glow. Sixty-five, Clay thought, and she still looks several steps beyond tremendous.

His wife sighed and stirred the pot again. "Okay, how about this? If – for some remote, to me unfathomable reason – you should die tonight, I'll take the photos to the drugstore tomorrow morning."

Clay smiled and said nothing.

"Well, if you're determined to go, I need some cotton balls and facial tissue. And go to CVS instead of Walgreen's. They're nicer to the elderly, especially if you get confused."

"I'm not going to be confused. I know exactly what I want," Clay said as he opened the door to the garage.

Just before he closed it, Betsy called out, "And it's a CD, Clayton, not a DVD. I only tell you that so you won't embarrass yourself."

Clay arrived back at the house an hour later, carrying a small plastic CVS bag.

Betsy looked up from the kitchen counter where she was slicing the now-cooled fudge. "Did you get the things I asked for?"

He closed his eyes, took a deep breath, and let it out. "No, hell no, I forgot." He stomped through the kitchen, shrugged out of his raincoat, and tossed it at one of the dining room chairs. It promptly slid to the floor. Then he slammed the bag down on the table which was still covered with photographs.

Betsy followed him into the dining room. "What's made you so grumpy? It's not a big deal. I can get them tomorrow."

"It's not the cotton balls," Clay said, trying hard not to let his frustration show. It was frustration, wasn't it, and not simply self-pity? "I couldn't get the damned machine to work, so a couple of the female clerks said they'd do it for me while I looked around."

They'd been college age, he thought, and cute, too – a slender redhead and a perky blonde. And he'd been grateful for their help until he'd heard their whispered voices from an adjacent aisle.

"They were giggling and talking while they did the processing – said it was pathetic – said things like 'I can't believe these photos are of him' – and 'God, please don't let me get old.'"

"Well, that's too bad. Someday they'll probably have to forgive themselves their youth. At least they didn't know what the pictures were for."

Clay closed his eyes again and bowed his head.

"Oh my God," Betsy said. "You told them didn't you?" She walked over and began massaging Clay's shoulders.

The intimacy of Betsy's action took some of the sting out of his pity party. Her touch had always helped restore him, becoming even more precious to him now for the infrequency of it.

She continued the massage with one hand while she poked around the pile of photographs on the table. "Look at this one, Clayton."

Clay opened his eyes. She had pulled out a photo of the two of them, taken when they were in their twenties. They sat on a deck railing, drinks of some kind in their hands. She was smiling while Clay sneered and raised his middle finger at the camera. "Jesus," she said. "I look like a bleached blonde from Charlotte."

He turned his head to look up at her. "You were a bleached blonde from Charlotte."

Betsy grinned.

"I'm going to trash the CD," Clay said. "Instead, I'm going to put this photo on a continuous loop. It'll be me giving the finger to the world, then fade to black, then me giving the finger again. What do you think of that?"

"It's your funeral, Clayton. Do whatever you want."

He studied the print. "I looked pretty good there, too," Clay said. "Don't you think?"

She gave his shoulder one last squeeze and turned toward the kitchen. "Honey, you were the cat's ass."

Clay twisted in his chair to follow her retreat. "Still am."

She flipped him the bird over her shoulder.

It made him smile.

Superheroes

Irena Tervo

*L*iv salivated at the scent of steaming pita bread at Talal's, and she tried to shake off the chill from the low February temps.

This new Mediterranean restaurant was unknown, but at least there wouldn't be a half hour wait on a Friday night, unlike the TGIF and Ruby Tuesday they'd passed on Pleasant Valley Dr. They'd been at the school's art show for the last few hours and, inspired by the children's creative works, had developed a ravenous appetite.

Something seemed off with the restaurant, but Liv couldn't articulate what it was.

Her husband, Jeff, raised his eyebrows at the lack of clientele, but that didn't really bother Liv. Most people she knew tended to be wary of new places, but gastronomically Liv was adventurous. She loved being the first to discover something exciting, and she didn't want her children to be the types that frequented the same boring places again and again. Women tended to change when they became mothers. They became germaphobes, paranoid and overprotective, teaching their children not to trust the world they lived in or the people around them.

The hostess of Talal's, a girl with mousy brown hair, greeted them with a slight bow. She pushed her thick horn-rimmed glasses up on her nose, gathered four menus and led them past the only occupied table in the restaurant, where an elderly couple was paying their bill.

They passed a sliding glass door leading out to a patio. Icicles drooped from the roof but tables were set, as if expecting to be filled, a hookah pipe placed on each one. Did people actually smoke them? Liv wondered, then decided they must be decorative. Just in case, she made a mental note to check it out before coming back with her kids when the weather got warmer. She was all for being adventurous, but exposing her kids to a terrace filled with smoke was another matter entirely.

The back room was deserted. Thick, shiny fabric lined the wall, lending the room an imposing air.

Ten-year old Caleb and six-year old Selma whined with hunger. The waitress appeared, ready to take their order. Gratefully, Liv scanned the menu, choosing an assortment of food for her family. Chicken kebobs and lamb. Pita and rice, hummus and falafels. As the waitress sprinted to the kitchen, a series of screams erupted as Caleb and Selma started a pinching war.

"Whoa," Jeff said while taking off his cardigan. "Is this the way my superheroes treat each other?" Ever the peacemaker, he pointed to his own Superman t-shirt. Jeff was like that, a boy at heart, who still subscribed to comics. Working as an engineer during the workweek, over the weekend he secretly longed to be more.

"Dad," Caleb said, "why do Superhero's need a secret identity?"

"Why do you think they would?" Jeff said.

Caleb's face was thoughtful. "Is it to protect their talent?"

"I like that answer."

Caleb grabbed a small placard at the center of the table. He squinted at the smallish letters and mouthed a few words. "Hey," he said. "They have comedy night here on Thursday's."

Selma made a grab for it. "Let me read it."

Thankfully, the waitress returned with steaming plates of food. Caleb released the calendar and Selma gave the waitress an angelic smile.

"Does this say belly?" Selma pointed to the calendar, proud she could spell the word on her own.

"Belly dancing." Caleb's eyes lit up. "It says you have belly dancing tonight. Where is it?"

The waitress pushed up her thick horn-rimmed glasses. "Let me ask my manager."

But Liv saw no dancers. The place was completely deserted, devoid of customers, save for them. Nervously, Liv scooped up her hummus. She wondered if she should follow the waitress and tell her not to bother. Or was she just being paranoid, like the other moms that frustrated her? Jeff divided up the kid's portions, giving each child three pieces of chicken and half the rice. He then began to attack his shish kebob.

The soft background music shut off abruptly. In that agitated silence, the bottom of Liv's stomach dropped. A blaring horn sounded in the speakers. It was an insistent sound, like a warning.

The lights dimmed.

A young girl undulated towards them.

Her green bikini was scant and gem studded, with beads that swished. Hair pulled back tightly on her head like a genie, her pale stomach rippled in staggered movements. The stomach was like a convulsing moon traveling around them with no command of itself. Agitating without purpose, beads rattled as hips shunted awkwardly.

Liv and Jeff struggled for the appropriate course of action, but this dancer was young, a novice, and neither of them wanted to hurt her feelings. Caleb's jaw widened in mid-chew, a piece of chicken stuck on his tongue. Selma looked frightened, as if she had the impulse to run.

Liv prayed the song would end soon.

The pipe played on, and it was like the sound of a slow, bleating goat strung up between two trees to be sacrificed. The dancer tried to be provocative, but came off self-conscious, which made the whole thing so much worse.

Liv felt she should do something to cut the whole thing short. She didn't want her son turning into one of those perverted men right in front of her eyes ... but she had no idea how to handle it in a polite way. The longer the notes played on, the more incompetent Liv felt. Liv pulled her cowl neck up for protection, as if she were a turtle submerging in its shell. Where had this dancer come from? Had she been hiding in the kitchen?

When finally the music ended, the dancer gazed at them, her young eyes seeming to ask if they thought she was any good, and how good was she? Only Caleb clapped his hands in delight.

"Again!" he shouted.

Liv stood up. "Not today." And, because she thought she noted a flash of hurt in the dancer's eye, she added, "Thank you."

The dancer bowed and left. Letting out a deep, trapped breath, Liv finally felt some semblance of control over her family again, but the hummus slathered over the round falafels on her plate made her feel slightly nauseated.

Jeff asked for the bill. They all moved slow and zombie-like to leave. Liv looked around for the dancer as they went from the back room into the main room, but all she saw was that mousy hostess with the horn-rimmed glasses at her post. The young girl barely met their gaze, but Liv thought she detected a flash of mischief in her thickly lined eyes. Liv hugged Selma close, a shiver running through her.

Caleb gave the hostess a thumbs-up sign. "I give this place six stars out of five," he said loudly. As Jeff dug his car keys out of his pocket, Caleb lingered at the hostess podium, motioning for the hostess to lean closer. She pushed a clump of dark hair behind her ear. Caleb meant to whisper, but Liv heard every word.

"Don't worry. Your secret is safe with me."

In Due Season

Douglas Wyant

Jody dreamed he was drowning. As he struggled to reach the surface, he heard a persistent knock, like a boat bumping against a dock. Gasping for air, he opened his eyes.

Dust motes floated in a sunbeam. Lifting a slat in the blinds, Jody peered out. All he saw was the back of a man's head. Cameron?

Jody pulled on cutoff blue jeans and a T-shirt emblazoned with an antiwar slogan: *Make love, not war*. He glanced back at the bed and then opened the door that separated his living quarters from the art gallery. He closed the inside door, walked through the gallery, and unbolted the outside door. The light in Jody's eyes dimmed and the smile on his face faded.

"Good morning. My name's Burk." The man held out a snapshot of a strawberry blonde. "I'm looking for this girl."

She looked like a dozen other college coeds Jody had seen that summer – freckled face, blue eyes, bouffant hair-do.

"She sent me this postcard last week," Burk said.

Jody scanned the message scrawled on the back of one of his island sketches.

"I've already been to Bonaparte's Retreat," Burk said. "No one seems to have seen her since lunch yesterday."

Jody circled the room, opening blinds. A whitewashed bell tower rose above the rusting tin roofs of a few rainbow-colored cottages, and a gray, ramshackle restaurant stood on stilts at the water's edge like an awkward, earthbound bird.

Burk frowned at an unframed canvas that looked as if the artist had cleaned his brushes on it. "I don't like abstract art. It seems too impersonal to me."

"People don't appreciate what they don't understand," Jody said. "This is a portrait of my brother Cameron. Eighteen months separate us, but it didn't seem to matter when we were growing up – best friends, fierce enemies, brothers – on a farm ten miles from our nearest neighbors."

Jody surprised himself, suddenly sharing secrets with this stranger, secrets he had hidden from friends. "The spring I was eleven, Cameron shoved me out of an apple tree. He roamed the woods alone, armed with a slingshot, while I spent the summer reading on the back porch, my left leg propped up on a kitchen chair. Every Saturday, on her way to the grocery store, Mom stopped by the public library to select a stack of boyhood biographies of famous Americans illustrated with silhouettes.

"That's how I started – cutting silhouettes out of black construction paper. Now, here I stand in my own studio." Jody gestured to his right. "And this is a painting of my mother."

A stout brunette stood with her back to them, staring out a window. A baby with bright eyes peered over the woman's left shoulder. A photograph of a young man in uniform hung above a small table. An empty envelope and a crumpled telegram lay on the table beside an open Bible. A verse from Ecclesiastes was engraved across the bottom of the painting: *To everything there is a season, a time for every purpose under heaven.*

Burk stepped closer to examine blocks of red and black letters on the woman's print dress. A single word, duplicated innumerable times, swam into focus – BATAAN.

"Dad was captured by the Japanese in 1942. Although released by American Marines in 1945, he was a POW the rest of his life. He supplemented his small government pension by selling fruit and vegetables and eggs from the tailgate of his pickup." Jody pointed to a small sketch of a gaunt man in bib overalls, surrounded by bags and boxes of produce, peeling an apple. His head was down, his face obscured by a straw hat.

"When the war in Vietnam flared up, Cameron enlisted, in spite of Dad's protests. I thought he looked splendid in his dress uniform, but the next time I saw him he was dressed in a bloody flight suit, being driven like a beast through a village in North Vietnam. That same day, Dad borrowed a gun from a neighbor to kill a hawk, he said, that was preying on his chickens."

The ferry whistle blew one long blast.

On his way out the door, Burk said, "When you see Sherry, tell her I'll look her up when I get back from Vietnam."

The ferry whistle blew two short blasts.

Jody watched the ferry back away from the pier. The door to his living quarters eased open. A petite, strawberry blonde peeked out.

NONFICTION

Photo by Jayne Bowers

Inner Critics

Barbara V. Evers

*T*he snort distracts me, and I stop writing and wait for the onslaught. The offender, a dragon-morph-unicorn, shakes his head, smoke streaming from his nostrils. "This is stupid."

"Is it?" I study the passage, doubt seeping into my mind. It sounds good to me, but dragon-morph has my attention. "I like it."

"You would." He continues reading over my shoulder, the heat of his breath fanning against my neck. "Did you really want to use that verb?"

I flush. From heat? From uncertainty?

"Well … at least the verb is active, not passive."

I wanted a different verb but decided to let it go for now. Sometimes, when I leave things alone, let them stew, the right word emerges like a flower after the rain.

"It's rather bland." My chair teeters as the dragon's massive, scaly tail swishes back and forth.

"Let me see." A female voice interrupts.

Oh no, he's morphed into the unicorn. She rarely speaks, she just —

Yep, there she goes. She laughs.

Not with you.

At you. A high-pitched whinny.

Her form flickers back and forth between dragon and unicorn, uable to control its shape during extreme mirth. I hate it when they gang up on me like this.

Shaking my shoulders, I try to shove them away and attempt to keep writing, but the verb taunts me. Should I change it?

"It needs to be stronger," the dragon recommends. "Get a thesaurus."

"Too much trouble." The heavy thesaurus lives in the other room. Instead, I right-click on the verb and check the synonym options suggested by Word.

Photo by Volker von Domarus
123rf.com

"How'd you do that?" The dragon blinks in surprise at my technical expertise, and I smile to myself, regaining the upper hand.

Of course, the feeling lasts a short moment.

"Tsk, a bit lazy aren't we?"

Which one said that? Have they finally merged into one? A dragocorn or unigon?

I keep writing.

"It's not like you'll get this published." The dragon jumps onto the keyboard, adding unwanted words and letters to my work. He taunts me as he points out the unworthy plot and word choices. I highlight and delete. Reword. Shift sentences.

He laughs and breathes fire onto the screen. I slap at him, trying to rescue the words – my words. Disgusted, I thump him across the room. He shivers, then shifts back into the unicorn.

She flickers in and out, but at least, she's content to stay quiet, settled in a corner, ignoring me. Maybe she's lost interest.

I re-read the questionable passage again. Glance at her. A light snuffle sounds as she breathes the sleep of the contented. I deem the words acceptable for now and try to move on.

With any luck, the unicorn will take a *long* nap.

Photo by Gabor Palla
freeimages.com

Old Friendships Change

Barbara V. Evers

The long flat road of the South Carolina flatlands stretched out before me.

"So what do you dream about?"

I cut my eyes away from the road to glance at Julie, my best friend from high school. I hadn't seen her in twenty years. After years of failed attempts, we'd found time to spend together – a family vacation at Myrtle Beach.

Her face held that same look I remembered – inquisitive innocence. Funny, her strange, off-the-wall questions contributed to her charm at sixteen. Twenty years later, not so much.

Appearance-wise, she hadn't changed a lot – hair a bit shorter, a few wrinkles, and now, I was discovering, her conversation skills had, in certain ways, stayed the same as in high school.

How had I missed this all of these years? I glanced back at her anticipatory expression, and then refocused on the road, wondering how to respond to this question. The last twelve hours since she climbed off the plane with tons of baggage felt like an interrogation.

My husband and I had looked at all of that luggage and chuckled to ourselves. It's a week at the beach, just an over-commercialized, family beach. Not the Riviera. Half of her luggage lay in disarray on my den floor now. Silly me, to think we needed room for our luggage in the car, too.

"You're avoiding the question." Her admonishment held a tone of, what? Something I'd heard from my teenage daughters. Petulance?

"Come on, Julie, so many questions." I smiled at her. "Look at this scenery."

This part of South Carolina's landscape doesn't offer much, flat and unending, but I needed a diversion. I knew she might become fascinated since she had never ventured into this area of the state.

A true mid-westerner, everything about the South Carolina upstate had enthralled Julie in high school. When would the fog go away? When would the leaves turn? How can you ride a bike on so many hilly roads?

The questions ran endless then, and they appeared to do so, now.

"What are they growing?" she said.

I didn't have to look. The crops stretched as far as I could see along this stretch of road. "Probably tobacco."

"Oh." A note of disappointment rang in her voice. "I thought it might be cotton."

"Doubt it, but it could be beans or soy." I pointed to the opposite side of the road where a modest, two-story farm house sat next to the fields. "Looks like they have corn growing over there."

"I know what corn looks like."

"Just trying to help," I said, hoping to keep her off her never ending questions.

I checked my rearview for our other car, driven by my husband. Several of the kids had started out with Julie and me in the van. All but one, deserted us for the non-inquisition car. Our remaining trooper, 19-year-old Heidi, lay in the back seat asleep.

What clues over the last 20 years of correspondence had I missed that might warn me this vacation together might prove a mistake?

When Julie had moved to South Carolina during high school, she broke barriers. People who never spoke to each other became her friends, and, likewise, friends to each other. I found her questions clever then, off the wall, but clever. People always answered her. The questions brought them together. Experience a silence in the group, awkward or not, and Julie filled it with a nonsensical question.

The guys loved her. She dated a lot that year until she met Duane. After that, other guys tried, but Duane held her heart. Me? I had few dates in high school. It didn't matter. My best friend was Julie, my claim to fame.

"Mom?" Heidi sat up in her seat, peering between sleepy lids. She yawned. "Are we there, yet?"

The infamous trip question. "Nope."

She sat up straighter and looked around at the farm land. "I gotta pee."

"Me too, baby, me too." I laughed at the joy of commonplace conversation and the surprise on Julie's face. "I think there's a town ahead. We'll stop there."

"Is there a rest area in the town?" Julie said.

"Nope." I stifled a laugh over her city and major interstate ideas. "But they'll have gas stations or maybe a McDonald's or something."

"Oh." Julie hesitated for a breath. "You know so much."

"What? You're the doctor." I tried to keep my jaw from hanging open.

"Yeah, but I don't know what I'm looking at out this window, and I'd panic if a kid told me she needed to pee with no bathroom in sight."

"Hey." Heidi sounded indignant from the back seat.

In the rearview mirror, I caught her gaze and gave her the look. I'll bet she moves to the other car after we stop.

"Julie," I said, "it's no miracle. You just learn what you need to know or you learn from experience. You know that."

Heidi smirked in the back seat. She recognized my tone and appeared to enjoy knowing that her Mom's dear old high school friend was exasperating.

Note to self: never take an old friend on vacation when your only contact for the last twenty years has been letters and the occasional phone call.

I envisioned us at graduation, standing back to back like duelers. We started walking, only I soon stopped, and she walked all the way across the country. We were as different as those challenged duelers on a foggy, grey morning. I wouldn't kill her on this trip because our bond held stronger than that, but my family might.

We both had changed. She became a doctor, after all, a specialist. But my changes revealed the stark difference in our worlds. My changes reflected a different responsibility. A person, it appeared, she admired.

Imagine that.

Blizzard Conditions

Bob Strother

My Crown Vic slid to a halt under the granite portico of the Crystal Gateway Marriott, its windshield caked with a tenacious mix of snow and sleet we'd run into about twenty miles south of the Washington, DC, beltway. It was late afternoon, Saturday, March 12, 1993.

"*Finally,*" Vicki said, collecting her purse and the fast food bags and cups we'd accumulated on the way up.

I checked the dashboard clock. "We made better time than last year – eight hours and forty minutes."

"Seemed longer than that," Susan said from the backseat.

I glanced over my shoulder and smiled at my 19-year-old stepdaughter and her Columbia College roommate, Beth. The two girls had accompanied my wife and me on our annual pilgrimage to the Appalachian Regional Commission/Local Development District Conference.

"Well," I said, "now we're here. Welcome to Arlington."

A doorman approached. "Where did you folks come from?" he said as we clambered from the car, eyeing us as though we'd just stepped out of a flying saucer.

"South Carolina," I said.

"You drove all that way in this?" He gestured toward the snow-covered landscape.

"No, only the last few miles," I said, wondering why my answer appeared so far-fetched.

While I parked the car, Vicki and the girls checked us in. When I arrived at our room a few minutes later, Vicki handed me a dozen pink phone message slips.

I frowned. "Why are these people calling me. They should already be here."

"You're the conference chair this year. Maybe they have questions."

Before I could begin returning calls, the room telephone rang. It was Bill Sanders, the ARC staffer who handled most of the on-the-ground logistics for the conference.

"We need to talk," he said.

Five minutes later, in Bill's room, I got the bad news. Bill leaned forward in his chair, elbows resting on his knees. "A blizzard has engulfed the entire East Coast and most of the South. Except for a handful of people who arrived early, everyone else is completely snowed in. Interstates are closed. Airports are closed. Nothing is moving."

The conference typically drew about 350 participants – mostly politicians and staffers – from across the thirteen Appalachian states, running from New York to Mississippi. The event was more than simply a means of sharing information, it also provided the opportunity for local municipal officials to visit with and lobby their House and Senate members.

"How many are here?"

Bill thought for a moment. "About 30, give or take – maybe eight from the Board."

The Local Development District Board had one member representing each of the thirteen Appalachian states. We conducted much of our yearly business at the conference.

"So we have a majority?"

Bill nodded. "You're the conference chair, so it's up to you. Call the whole thing off, or plow through with what we have. Either way, I have to let the hotel know immediately, and the federal office, too."

The federal office of the ARC housed about 50 employees on Connecticut Avenue in DC. Many of them, especially the ones who dealt regularly with the development districts, participated in the conference. If they could come, it would add to our group, but we'd still be at less than fifteen percent of what we'd planned for – a dismal number to match my dismal mood. In less than a half hour, I had gone from eagerly anticipating the crowning achievement of my tenure as conference chair to feeling like a punctured balloon.

Bill slouched in his chair, waiting for my response. "For what it's worth," he offered, "nobody's leaving for home for at least a couple of days."

I hung my head – all that work, *my* work, for naught. Then I took a deep breath and sighed. "Let's do it."

As I was leaving, Bill said, "I'm sorry I had to dump this on you, but I have to ask – how did you not know what was happening?"

"The girls rented Dean Koontz's *Mr. Murder* on cassette tapes – the unabridged version. I never once turned on the car radio. We didn't see bad weather until we were just outside the Beltway."

Back in our room, Vicki told me that Dirk Reis, a staff member from my office, had called and wouldn't be coming. "Apparently the Charlotte airport was already closed when we breezed by it heading north on I-85."

"There're all closed," I said. "The storm must have been coming up our tailpipes the whole way."

"Your mom called," Vicki said. "She's been praying for us since early this morning. My dad called, too." She grinned. "He's been cussing you about the same amount of time for risking all our lives."

I'd have prayed, too, if I'd known of the tempest following us up the interstate. As it was, I had to settle for spouting my own impotent epithets at a smirking Mother Nature.

We gathered the girls and rode the elevator down to the mall below the hotel where we found the subway station and most of the shops and restaurants closed and gated due to the weather. Fortunately, the Hamburger Hamlet was still open, and we went in for food and much-needed drinks.

It was there I came across the first and only piece of good luck I'd had since arriving. In the booth adjacent to us, Patsy Cline sat having dinner with a man I didn't recognize. She wasn't really Patsy, but she was the next best thing – Kaye Crow, who had headlined the play, *Always, Patsy Cline,* at Greenville's Little Theater. Vicki and I had attended her performance, loved her right away, and I subsequently contracted with her and her band to provide the entertainment for the conference's main banquet.

"Kaye," I said, "you made it."

She smiled and introduced me to her husband. "David and I came early to do some sightseeing. Unfortunately, the band didn't make it."

"Would you still perform if we can find a band for you?"

"We'd have to practice some," she said, "but … sure, if you can arrange it."

"Let me see what I can do."

On our way back to the elevator, we stopped at one of the mall exits. Outside, a thick, horizontal curtain of wind and snow swept past, rattling the glass doors like a runaway train.

"It's so beautiful," Susan said. "I've *got* to get out in it."

"Me, too." echoed Beth.

"Not me," I said. Then both girls burst through the opening, and we were almost lifted off our feet by a blast of frigid air.

We watched as Susan and Beth did pirouettes in the driving snow, then held hands and skipped around the small outdoor courtyard like ten-year-olds. A freezing minute later they returned, red-cheeked and soaked to the skin but near hysterical with laughter.

"Come on," Vicki said, taking my hand.

"Are you joking? We'll freeze to death."

She opened the door again and dragged me out behind her. "So what if we do? At least you won't have to worry about the conference."

The cold smacked us in the face, the wind fluttered our clothes like torn sails, and wet snow plastered our hair to our heads. Vicki grabbed my other hand, and we circled slowly in an awkward and slippery arctic waltz. It felt silly at first, but maybe it was cathartic. A minute later, we rejoined the girls inside, half-frozen – as I had predicted – but for a moment, at least, distracted from my wreck of a conference.

I attended meetings all day Sunday, staring forlornly out at near-empty rooms, and generally feeling sorry for myself. The Metro had cranked up again, and Vicki and the girls went sightseeing despite the fact none of them had packed clothes appropriate for the late winter snowstorm. They'd begun at the Smithsonian and traveled as far as the Viet Nam Memorial, where the girls had made charcoal rubbings.

"The park workers drove metal poles into the ground all across the National Mall," Vicki said, "and strung rope through them to help people navigate through the snow. The cool thing was – there were no lines to get in anywhere."

The banquet was held that evening, and after all the speeches were over, Kaye Crow and her last-minute, put-together band performed a wonderful medley of Patsy Cline hits for a meager but highly appreciative audience.

I had more meetings and workshops the following morning, and when I returned to my room on a break, Vicki was lying on the bed reading a magazine.

"How was breakfast?" I asked

"Great."

"And lunch?"

"Absolutely wonderful," she said, stretching.

"Really? What'd you have?"

"Filet mignon."

"You had a filet for lunch?"

She grinned. "Breakfast, too. Seems the hotel ordered over three hundred of them for some conference that didn't pan out. So they decided to share some of them with us on the Concierge Level. The girls and I had a grand feast before they went back out on the Metro."

"Well," I said, trying hard but unsuccessfully to control my growing frustration, "I'm glad you and the girls are having such tremendous fun. Meanwhile, I'm presiding over the sinking of the Titanic."

We did *not* have filets for dinner that evening, but instead feasted on burgers and pasta from Hamburger Hamlet, my pain slowly ebbing as the doomed conference neared its welcome end.

On Tuesday morning, after I attended one final meeting, we packed our belongings and headed south. It was only then, while listening to NPR, I learned the true impact of what came to be known as the Blizzard of '93.

The storm had come up through the Gulf of Mexico, producing hurricane-force winds, storm surges, and tornados, wreaking havoc from as far south as Cuba all the way to Canada. The

Photo by Edith Hawkins

southern states and the East Coast suffered record cold temperatures, ten million people lost power, and over 300 died from storm-related causes.

Vicki turned the volume down. "Wow, it's hard to believe we were having such a great time while so many people were suffering."

"You and the girls were having a great time," I reminded her. "But you're right. It does sort of put my situation in perspective."

I ruminated about that a lot during our trip back to South Carolina. We were lucky compared to many in the storm's wake. There had never been a question about our survival. I had worked through my own ordeal, felt vastly relieved now that it was over, and was traveling home bent but not broken.

I looked over at my beautiful wife, caught a glimpse of the two lovely girls currently napping in the back seat, and decided I was, in fact, a fortunate man to have all I had, regardless of whatever problems I might encounter in the future.

It occurred to me then the most important thing wasn't merely the fact we had survived the storm – we had also danced in the snow.

Getting There

William Thrift

Sometime during my sophomore year in high school I realized I was intrigued by girls. I respected them, even revered them to the point of being mortified around them.

I grew ever-hyperconscious of my conduct and appearance in their presence. These emotional barriers led me down a quirky path. Afraid that I might embarrass myself, I reserved responses in class for when I had particularly obscure answers (that I thought girls might remember and associate with the tall, quiet boy). I was meticulous about my grooming and dress, even though I didn't possess the means for clothes with the tiny, conspicuous logos on them – little alligators, embroidered horses and such. I wore anonymous pants and hand-me-downs from prior decades, occasionally a sweater or shirt I had gotten for Christmas. But I was still too young to recognize, let alone lament, my economic reality. I took it in stride and made the best of what I had.

At least that was the case until the day when two circumstances occurred that caused my thoughts on girls and money to converge. I know now that you can find happiness without money, and you shouldn't need money to attract a companion. But the depths of those considerations were yet to be found in the shallow pool of my 15-year-old mind.

Pam was a classmate, a girl for whom I had a mild attraction. One afternoon I sat in a booth with her in the McDonald's across Augusta Road from school. She and her younger brother were waiting on their father to pick them up. I knew she had to do this on occasion and had made something of a habit of sitting with her.

While we talked about this and that, Pam took a fold of cash out of her purse and told her brother to get her a Coke and whatever drink he wanted for himself. She didn't ask me if I wanted anything. Maybe she assumed I didn't. Maybe she assumed I had my own money (which I didn't) and I'd get something to drink if I wanted it.

Despite my presence on these afternoons at McDonald's (and it was easy to read that my company was welcome), we didn't kindle the kind of relationship I thought might be possible between us. We were friends, and we both seemed to be okay with that notion.

But there was a nobler reason in the back of my mind for sitting with her in that public place. I knew kids from public school hung out at McDonald's. We Christian school students were often the target of their insults and ridicule, and I didn't want Pam to bear that alone should it happen at all. I wanted to protect her and take care of her, and for some reason I began to associate that ideal with her father and the cash he had given her, no doubt, to help her pass the time.

If I had been able to treat her to a Coke, maybe she would think of me as more than a friend. Maybe that small gesture would have sparked the romance between us we were otherwise resigned to dismiss. Thinking back on it, the potential for what she and I could be was part of what attracted me to her.

Besides, it made me thirsty watching her sip at her Coke (and thirstier knowing I couldn't buy one for myself). Then her father came, and I walked back across Augusta and down Cureton toward home.

Along the way, I saw an acquaintance riding his bike. Andy hailed me and pedaled over. He was a year older than I, and lived in the neighborhood. We spoke, but not often. So he made some small talk with me and then got down to it.

"You ever done a paper route before?"

"No." I had no idea why he would ask me such a thing.

"How would you like to take over mine for a few weeks?"

I caught myself before answering "sure." A paper route was not just some mindless job. It was a commitment. There were customers involved, and they had to get their papers in the morning no matter what. But no doubt there would be payment for my services. Opportunity was knocking.

I asked, and Andy filled me in about the details. His route was for only the weekday morning edition. He had already paid his distributor for three weeks' worth. He also had all of the rubber bands I'd need for the job and he'd loan me his pouch. He'd be making collections from his subscribers, so I didn't have to worry about that.

It all sounded so professional – distributors, subscribers, collections. Where else could a 15-year-old get such a job? So I agreed to do it.

He told me to meet him at a certain corner across Farris Road at five a.m. the next morning to show me the route. "And don't be late. We've got to fold 'em and deliver 'em before sunrise."

I liked the stealth of the paper route – getting up in the pre-dawn darkness, dressing quickly and quietly so as not to disturb the rest of the household, mounting my ten-speed, and click-shifting away down Cureton toward Farris Road and the rendez-vous point with some guy in a station wagon – whoever-he-was. Let's say he was from HQ and I was a spy. He'd drop off a bundle of papers on the curb.

Kneeling in a cone of streetlight, I would tri-fold and rub-ber-band all fifty copies in less than ten minutes. Andy had shown me how to do this, and I enjoyed the economy of movement – fold, fold, hook index finger in rubber band, pull the band over the folded paper, and place in a neat stack. Then I had to cram all fifty into the canvas bag. Why Andy's bag wasn't just a little bit bigger was beyond me. Wednesday editions were the worst with all the coupons and inserts.

I hefted the awkward bag over my head so it hung across my chest and back. At first it was tough steering with a full bag. I had to use a combination of gravity and certain body contortions (depending upon the angle of the bike and the road) to keep from wrecking. Having to ride in and out of the alternating darkness and light from the overhead street lamps didn't help. Somewhere between fifteen and twenty deliveries, steering became more manageable. By then I was in a groove, pedaling down streets and coasting at a tilt around corners.

Andy had given me a list of street names – in geographical order from the drop point – that comprised his route. Instead of giving me the addresses of each house on his route, he showed me which houses on each street didn't get the morning paper (there were only a handful).

By the time the sky lightened and the route was nearing completion, my eyes had adjusted, and I felt energized. At first I dreaded the early hours, thinking I would be dragging all day. But I found the opposite to be true. I was more alert in my morn-ing classes. I wasn't somnolent after lunch. Before the route I'd struggled to keep my eyes open. I'd like to think that even my grades improved during this time. I seem to recall a couple of perfect scores on quizzes, as though the black smudges of the printed words that marred my clothes, my bike, and various surfaces at home had indeed soaked through my skin to augment my brain. I was benefitting by being a link in the information chain, a part of the larger industry of knowledge.

Andy said he'd pay me at the end of the three weeks. The day he handed me seventy-five dollars was the day my ship tacked in a new direction. I no longer had to float in tow, astern of a beaten man whose own ship was doomed. Instead of languishing in the downward spiral that had been life with my father, I looked ahead and saw light. For the first time I could recall, my future wasn't blotted out. I began to perceive the inception of a plan – actions that would lead to prosperity. I could add value to my life, and I could do it by pedaling my bike as far as my legs would take me.

I decided to reward myself for my efforts by improving my wardrobe. But despite my desire to sport new fashion, I was frugal with my newfound wealth. I rode all the way to McAllister Square where I shunned the big department stores and found in a discount store a pair of khaki pants and a yellow button-down oxford that just screamed springtime. I had 58 dollars to spare and started carrying eight of them in a cracked wallet I'd gotten for my tenth birthday. The rest was hidden in my room in a place only I knew.

I wore my new outfit to school with my wallet buttoned into my back pocket. I felt in those brief three weeks like I had transcended a space-time portal. I was a new person. I stood a little taller when the entire school assembled for daily chapel. I sang hymns with more gusto, and I caught the eye (or thought I did) of not a few of my female classmates.

Pam and I remained friends, but I didn't sit with her at McDonald's anymore. I'd like to think that my modest new wardrobe played a part in luring another girl, Susan, to cast a provocative look my way. But it was I who took the bait. While I chatted with her between classes, I began to think I might need that new pair of penny loafers I'd spied at Thom McAn's.

Later that day, as fate would have it, Andy told me of a kid he knew who had broken his leg and whose dad was desperate to get out of fulfilling his son's newspaper delivery commitment. The route was farther away than Andy's, but I knew I could get there every morning if I rode fast enough.

POETRY

Photo by Edith Hawkins

A Tree's Lament to Winter

Torie Amarie Dale

He dances into my world on the wind
Swirls around me with abandon

I hold my ground, steadfast, steady, sure
He can't budge me with his wicked whispering
Can't move me with his stormy moods

Nevertheless, he strips me of my dignity
Leaving me with me nothing but my naked needs

He laughs when the children play in the
Scattered remnants of who I used be

Photo by Edith Hawkins

Let Me be Your Water

Vickie Gregg

Ice, to deny you.

Steam, to singe the tips of your anger.

Cool and flowing, to quench your inner thirst.

Warm and wet, to receive your nakedness,

Your splashing, your play.

I will restore you.

Let me be your water.

Photo by Michael Hugh Lythgoe

My Naked Bones

Vickie Gregg

The naked bones of my body
Lie stripped and broken waiting
For you to mend them with
The flesh of your arms, your hands.

The naked bones of my body
Lie exposed on the bed.
Open nerves tingle at your need,
Begging your instinctive pursuit.

The naked bones of my body
Cry out from their inner sanctuary
Of desire, sequestered
Six feet under my skin.

The naked bones of my body
Find you, yielding inside me,
Pulse on pulse, breath on breath,
Adorning me in flesh.

A Boy is Like a Pony

Will Jones

A boy is like a pony, of course.
Trots, whinnies, and only stops
When he is a little hoarse

Spring grows him with its magic source.
Running, rolling, green-streaked tail to top,
A boy is like a pony, of course

BB gun becomes a moral force.
Warm bird in palm lays still. Tears drop
Til he is a little hoarse.

Stallion games: rear and rassle. Biting is too coarse,
And Mom stings flanks, switch for a crop.
A boy is like a pony, of course.

Girls make him gawky. So he roars
And jumps from behind trees - they want to talk.
Suddenly, he is a little hoarse.

He gallops two-beat, not in fourths,
And shakes a mane that looks more the wet mop.
A boy is like a pony, of course,
When he is a little hoarse.

THE CATAWBA
Nan Lundeen

shape me –

peace pipe
horse pot
turtle jar

I know
your old hands

I breathe
people of the river

down at your
sacred place
claim me
from the riverbank

dig and wash
strain and dry me

wet and roll and pinch and rub

hold me

shuddering under your river-rock

a hundred years old

from over there

handed down from mother

to son

from great-grandmother

to daughter

to son

stroke and smooth and burnish and sheen

buried in fire, I

create shape

like hands and toes and bellies and brains

in a woman's womb

through fire I carry form

remembering old hands

Photo by Michael Hugh Lythgoe

The Weight of Winter

Michael Hugh Lythgoe

The oak men come to town,
render trauma care, crippled trees down.
Minnesota arborist in tree-climbing gear
growls his saw in hard hat, calls out *timber*.
Tree surgeon deconstructs surface cuts.

In late winter comes another
fracture, dark plates rub together,
loud tremor, earth shakes, more
than plus four on the Richter scale,
fault line in bedrock near Savannah River.

Appalachians continue to erode, bridges
stay safe. Nuclear facilities unbroken.
Unholy wreckage all around. Woods
feel like artillery cut them down.
Steel beams, skeletal shell ascends

to enclose new tabernacle, church, stone
keep, bell tower; burden of winter cracks
a pine tree's spine. Winter is bone
cold, a snap, sleet gives pilgrims pain,
bent sycamores retain the will to stand.

Only ghost trees remain. Ravaged penitents
line the path to Ash Wednesday. For Lent
ice atones, melts, ashes mark a crow,
even as a handful of cold daffodils huddle
on a corner; a crow calls out a pothole.

Troubles underground; the world's old woes
murmur like widows in black sunning
in decimated parks; dreams of rings, missing
life lines open as log ends leave, pass pears,
trees in new buds. Spring in bridal white appears.

Photo by Michael Hugh Lythgoe

Photo by *Michael Hugh Lythgoe*

Pilgrim Beach

Michael Hugh Lythgoe

> *Give me my scallop-shell of quiet,*
> *...*
> *And thus I'll take my pilgrimage.*
> — Sir Walter Raleigh

This morning the horizon is lonely.
No ships to be seen. Atlantic empty.
A light blue sky is also free,
cloudless, swept clean; slowly
an egret-white smear glides south.
But one is never alone
in the Gulf Stream; Neptune's
waves keep trying to reach someone;

breakers end in froth & spume,
fall to their knees like priests in Holy Week,
go prone on the sand, to atone? God knows?
Whitecaps, gone. Sun enlightens horizontal
path to emptiness; pilgrim sees absence glisten.
A scallop shell fulfills a vertical soul.

Callaloo

Michael Hugh Lythgoe

After squalls I seek the taste of soup: calalloo.
Hurricane Ivan shivers church timbers.Simple soup
heals islanders on Carricou.

St. George rises on flanks of harbor, in tiers.
Forts nest above carenage, Sendall Tunnel.
Grenada, West Indies beckons divers.

In 1961 a cruise ship drowns:
Bianca C, burns; a clean reef forms
from wreck alive with octopus, green morays.

Circular children encrusted in coral, sculptures;
Divers swim with barracuda, free of plastic,
no pollution; tourists leave no bottles, light intruders.

Calypso – Spice Mas Carnival –
parade, steel drums at Tanteen, Lagoon Road;
songs in shade of Scots Kirk, Market Hall.

O let me return some day to Kick 'em Jenny
Channel, the cliff, to hear again the ghosts
of Arawak jumpers leap into history.

Please let me kneel in the Catholic Cathedral, feel
lumber tropical storms exposed; poor souls.
O Lord, may calalloo soup & votive candle

redeem me. Let me view cascades, cataracts,
Calabash, Mount St. Catherine, Paraclete.
The recipe for Calalloo is a contract

to cook greens & okra, crab meat, limes,
pepper, thyme, coconut milk, sweet potato,
shrimp, pear avocado. Place to dine?

Chez Bamboo. Have Tamarind Chicken Wings.
See the ketch sail in, owned by actor-sailor-
philanthropist. Praise Caribe chefs, sing.

Give thanks. Say grace at the Bath & Turtle.
Rice & peas. Let our visit do no harm.
Help us grow nutmeg & mace, below volcano.

TPR
JUDGES

FICTION

Photo by Barbara V. Evers

Phillip DePoy

PHILLIP DEPOY began his work as a writer in 1965 with the Actors and Writers Workshop. Ten years later he had become a published poet and acquired a masters degree in performance art. Soon thereafter he became a writer in residence for the Georgia Council for the Arts and a nationally reviewed performance artist. In the 1980s he was the composer in residence for the Academy Theatre. In the 1990s he was the Artistic Director of Theatrical Outfit, a professional Equity theatre. Since then he has served as the director of several university theatre programs. His Flap Tucker mysteries are published at Dell (one was a Shamus finalist), the Fever Devilin novels are from MacMillan who also published his stand alone novel, *The King James Conspiracy*, (translated into Chinese, Greek, and Portuguese). Non-fiction work includes *The Tao and the Bard* from Arcade/Skyhorse. There have been forty-seven productions of his plays, including the Edgar Award winning *Easy*, best mystery play of 2002, and *Appalachian Christmas Homecoming*, produced throughout the United States. Two new mystery series are in the offing for 2015, including one featuring Christopher Marlowe, playwright and Queen's spy. The Tony Award winning Alliance Theatre will produce DePoy's new play, *Edward Foote*, in the spring of 2015.

" I have learned over the years that my perspectives are decidedly odd and certainly out of step. Add to that the fact that my opinions about writing are so subjective as to render them almost meaningless. I'm certain that I'm not an authoritative voice of any sort. That said, I find myself remarkably impressed by the writing in this volume; the work and the joy involved. "

Sheila Morris

SHEILA MORRIS is the author of three nonfiction books and her most recent is *I'll Call It like I See It: A Lesbian Speaks Out*. All three of her books were finalists in the Golden Crown Literary Society Awards for essays and her first book *Deep in the Heart: A Memoir of Love and Longing* won that award in 2008. She has a short story published in *the storyteller* magazine and a story included in the 2013 Texas Folklore Society anthology. She was born and raised in rural southeast Texas and is a graduate of the University of Texas in Austin. She has a master's degree from the University of South Carolina in Columbia where she has lived for more than forty years. Her current project is compiling oral histories of the activists in the GLBTQ movement in South Carolina for the period 1984-2014.

She blogs at: **redsrantsandraves. com, iwillcallit.com** and **sraemorris-photo.wordpress.com**

Her author website is **writersheilamorris.com.**

" I never cease to be amazed at the imagination of good fiction writers, and I thought the entries to this year's contest were excellent. The diversity of characters, places and plot made reading them an adventure. Congratulations to the winners! Keep writing, everyone! "

NONFICTION

Cara Blue Adams

CARA BLUE ADAMS' stories have appeared in *Narrative, The Sun, The Missouri Review, The Mississippi Review, The Kenyon Review, EPOCH,* and other magazines. She is the recipient of scholarships and fellowships to the Bread Loaf Writers' Conference, the Sewanee Writers' Conference, and the Virginia Center for the Creative Arts and has been named one of Narrative's '15 Below 30' and awarded the Missouri Review Peden Prize and the Kenyon Review Short Fiction Prize. She is an assistant professor of creative writing at Coastal Carolina University.

" A big congratulations to the nonfiction writers! Great work finds its place, and I'm so happy yours has found its way here and into the lucky hands of readers. "

James Borton

JAMES W. BORTON teaches teaches writing in the English and Marine Science Departments at Coastal Carolina University. He's a former foreign correspondent for *The Washington Times*, completing in-depth interviews with former Philippines President Fidel Ramos, Nur Misuari, the Muslim rebel leader and also Hun Sen, the Prime Minister of Cambodia. He writes on environmental issues and challenges associated with the Mekong River and is currently engaged in reporting on the Winyah Bay environment.

Borton's seminal book *Venture Japan: How Growing Companies Worldwide Can* Tap *into the Japanese Venture Capital Markets*, was published by Probus in January 1992. He recently edited *The Art of Medicine in Metaphors* (Copernicus Healthcare) 2013.

Borton holds both a B.A and a M.A with honors in English and American Studies from the University of Maryland, College Park, Maryland and has been a former National Endowment Fellow at Yale University. He has also been an active member of the President's Circle of The Asia Society in New York City and the Foreign Correspondents Club in Hong Kong.

He blogs at **allheartmatters.com** and sails out of Winyah Bay.

" Congratulations to all of the creative nonfiction writers. I thank all of you for allowing me to read your work. Each of you offers an identifiable singular voice in your essays, literary journalism and memoirs. This genre of narrative nonfiction can be best understood as the union of storytelling and journalism. In short we write 'the art of truth. I encourage all of you to continue to write your story. And if that's not enough, follow Emerson's advice: " Live in the sunshine, swim the sea, drink the wild air ... "

POETRY

Photo by Edith Hawkins

Gilbert Allen

GILBERT ALLEN lives with his wife, Barbara, on Paris Mountain, in upstate South Carolina. He is the author of six collections of poems: *In Everything, Second Chances, Commandments at Eleven, Driving to Distraction, Body Parts*, and *Catma*. In 2005 he edited the anthology *A Millennial Sampler of South Carolina Poetry*. His work has received The Robert Penn Warren Prize from *The Southern Review* and has been featured on *The Writer's Almanac* and *Verse Daily*. He is the Bennette E. Geer Professor of Literature at Furman University, and he was inducted into the South Carolina Academy of Authors in 2014.

" I often tell my Furman students that poetry gives those of us who can't sing something to do. I hope you've found joy in the writing and reading of poems, and I hope that joy remains with you – and with me – in the future."

Libby Bernardin

LIBBY BERNARDIN's chapbook, *The Book of Myth* was selected by Kwame Dawes as a winner of the 2009 South Carolina Poetry Initiative Contest, and Finishing Line Press published *Layers of Song* in 2011. Her poems have appeared in journals such as *Southern Poetry Review*, *The South Carolina Poetry Society Yearbook*, *Cairn*, *Kakalak* and *Cider Press Review*. She is the recipient of the 1986 South Carolina Arts Commission Fellowship. Bernardin is a member of the Poetry Society of South Carolina and of the Board of Governors of the South Carolina Academy of Authors.

Layers of Song

Libby Bernardin

" Thank you for the opportunity to read the poems that will grace... *The Petigru Review*. A task of being a part of a tribe, in this case a literary tribe, requires attention to our purpose. In a way, it is a sacred task – one we all share – this honing of our craft. What a privilege for me to read the works of these poets as they share their words and insights. Congratulations to all. "

Daniel Cross Turner

DANIEL CROSS TURNER (Ph.D., Vanderbilt) is Associate Professor of American Literature at Coastal Carolina University. He is the author of the scholarly book, *Southern Crossings: Poetry, Memory, and the Transcultural South* (Tennessee, 2012). His numerous articles appear in edited collections as well as journals including *Mosaic, Genre, Mississippi Quarterly, Southern Literary Journal,* and *Southern Quarterly.* With Eric Gary Anderson and Taylor Hagood, he is co-editing *Undead Souths: The Gothic and Beyond* for Louisiana State University Press. He is also co-editing an anthology of poetry for the University of South Carolina Press, titled *Hard Lines: Rough South Poetry.*

" For the poets: thanks and praises. I am honored, humbled that I was given to help in some small way to steward good poems onto the page, to thrive now out there in front of a live audience. John Berryman compared writing poetry to being nearly crucified. Let's hope it doesn't come to that. But anyone even loosely connected with poets and poetry knows how much they suffer to form their words, how much it hurts to string their hearts out along the lines. Charles Wright advised, "Take a loose rein and a deep seat." Bon courage outstrips bon voyage. Steady your good hearts. Write on. "

CONTRIBUTING

TORIE AMARIE DALE remembers being told as a child she descended from Irish royalty and her family's castle is still there, lying in ruins somewhere in Ireland. In fact, oral stories were a huge part of her childhood and helped to form her character and writing abilities. Her writing has been nominated for the Pushcart prize twice, won several awards, and was made into a short film. Torie is also a motivational speaker and teacher on the effects of domestic abuse. Part of that effort includes teaching sketch journaling classes monthly at her local domestic violence abuse shelter.

TorieAmarieDale.com

BARBARA V. EVERS loves books, whether reading them or writing them. She works as a professional trainer and public speaker, and in her spare time, pursues her passion for books. Barbara's short stories and essays have appeared in the best-selling anthology, *Child of My Child: Poems and Stories for Grandparents, The Petigru Review, the moonShine review,* and *Stupefying Stories.*

Barbara blogs at
AnEclecticMuse.blogspot.com and
TheWorkbenchofFaith.wordpress.com.

Photo by Michael Hugh Lythgoe

AUTHORS

Photo: Flickr ©JoelMontes

VICKIE GREGG is a collaboration of two award-winning authors whose love of poetry and rich language merged to create a few poems with a lyrical beauty that they feel will appeal to a wide audience of readers. They each have multiple published works with Vickie focusing primarily on creative writing and Gregg having many journalistic and feature pieces, as well as some creative non-fiction works.

WILSON LANFORD returned to her ancestral roots in South Carolina ten years ago after a career in the government, She spends her time traveling or enjoying her home, especially the kitchen, her garden and her four canine companions.

WILL JONES and family live in Aiken, SC. His poetry and short stories have been published in The Petigru Review and other collections. Will also writes songs, in which his 18-month-old grandson and budding co-writer delights.

CONTRIBUTING

NAN LUNDEEN is the author of *Black Dirt Days: Poems as Memoir* and *The Pantyhose Declarations*. Her poetry has appeared in the College of Charleston's *Illuminations*, *The Petigru Review*, *Yemassee Literary Journal*, *Iowa Writes*, and *The South Carolina Poetry Initiative*. Her columns on writing have appeared in the UK's *Writing Magazine*, the S.C. Writers Workshop *Quill*, and femalefirst.com. An award-winning journalist, she has written for the *Detroit News*, the *Grand Rapids Press*, *The Greenville News*, the *Connecticut Post* and others. She facilitates Moo of Writing workshops. Visit her at nanlundeen.com

RICHARD LUTMAN has a MFA in Writing from Vermont College. He teaches short story classes as part of Coastal Carolina University's Lifelong Learning program. His fiction has appeared in publications including *Epiphany Magazine*, *The Bethlehem Writers Roundtable* and *Prick of the Spindle*. He has also won awards for his short stories, nonfiction, and screenplays. He was a 2008 Pushcart nominee in fiction and the recipient of national awards for his non-fiction, short stories and screenplays. His first novel will be published in 2015.

MICHAEL HUGH LYTHGOE is a Hoosier by birth. He studied at The University of Notre Dame and St. Louis university, served as a career officer in the USAF, and later earned an MFA from Bennington College. He has lived in Aiken with his wife, Louise, since 2004. Mike has taught at USCA for the Academy For Lifelong Learning, and served as President. One of his current obsessions is herons. His poetry collection, *Holy Week*, is available as an ebook. He has two nominations for a Pushcart. Recent work appears in *Windhover, Christianity and Literature, Bluestreak, Cairn, Spillway, SixFold, Pea River, Innisfree, The Poetry Society of SC Yearbook of winning poems 2014*, and *The Petigru Review*.

As a teen, **JODIE CAIN SMITH** listened as her grandmother told the gripping story of her adolescence in 1930s rural Alabama and the murder trial that altered her life. The tale took root in Jodie's memory until at last it became *The Woods at Barlow Bend*, her debut novel to be released November 19, 2014, by Deer Hawk Publications. Holding a BFA in Theatre Arts and a Master's degree in education, Jodie's columns have appeared in *Chicken Soup for the Military Spouse's Soul, The Savannah Morning News, The Fort Hood Sentinel* and on her blog, thequeendom.org.

Award-winning author and two-time Pushcart Prize nominee **BOB STROTHER** has had over eighty short stories published. His collection, *Scattered, Smothered, and Covered*, was published in 2011, and his novel-in-stories, *Shug's Place*, was released in May of 2013. Bob was the recipient of the 2012 Hub City Writers/Emrys Foundation Fiction Prize. He was also featured in, and is a contributing writer for *Southern Writers Magazine*. Bob's short story "Doughnut Walk" published previously in *TPR*, was adapted for a short film in the 2014 Expecting Goodness Film Festival. Bob lives with his wife, Vicki, in Greenville, South Carolina.

IRENA TERVO writes YA, MG, picture books, short stories and articles. Her YA novel was awarded semi-finalist in the Novel-in-Progress category of The Pirate's Alley William Faulkner – William Wisdom 2013 competition and she was awarded first prize in the annual Hub City/ Emrys Creative Writing Contest in the Nonfiction category. Additionally, she has been published in *Edible Upcountry Magazine, The Petigru Review* and has won two Honorable Mention awards in *Writer's Digest Competitions*.

A graduate of the University of South Carolina, **WILLIAM THRIFT** has traveled extensively in the US and abroad. After serving many years as a corporate regional manager, his creative side has emerged. In addition to writing a novel, he has placed 2nd Runner-up in the 2011 and 2012 Pirate's Alley Faulkner Society's Faulkner – Wisdom Creative Writing Competition for his short stories: "The Summer of My Faith" and "And The Sun Sets On Walker Street." He has also been published in the *The Petigru Review*. He serves as Secretary for the historic Cottontown neighborhood in Columbia.

DOUGLAS WYANT was the recipient of the first SCWW Scott Lax Wildacres Scholarship in 2012. He has also received a first place Carrie McCray Memorial Literary Award for non-fiction and an honorary mention for fiction. His stories have been published in *The Petigru Review* and *moonShine review.*

PHOTOGRAPHERS

JAYNE BOWERS has published articles and stories in *Guideposts*, *The Petigru Review* and two LDS magazines, the *Liahona* and *the Ensign*. Jayne has written four books: *Human Relations in Industry*, *Musings of a Missionary Mom*, *Crossing the Bridge: Succeeding in a Community College and Beyond* and *Eve's Sisters*.

BARBARA V. EVERS is a professional trainer and public speaker, and in her spare time, pursues her passion for books.

EDITH HAWKINS is a member of the Chapin Writer's Group. Her first book, *Summer Adventures with Kate & JR*, was published in 2013. She shares her love of photography and gardening through the creation of photo cards.

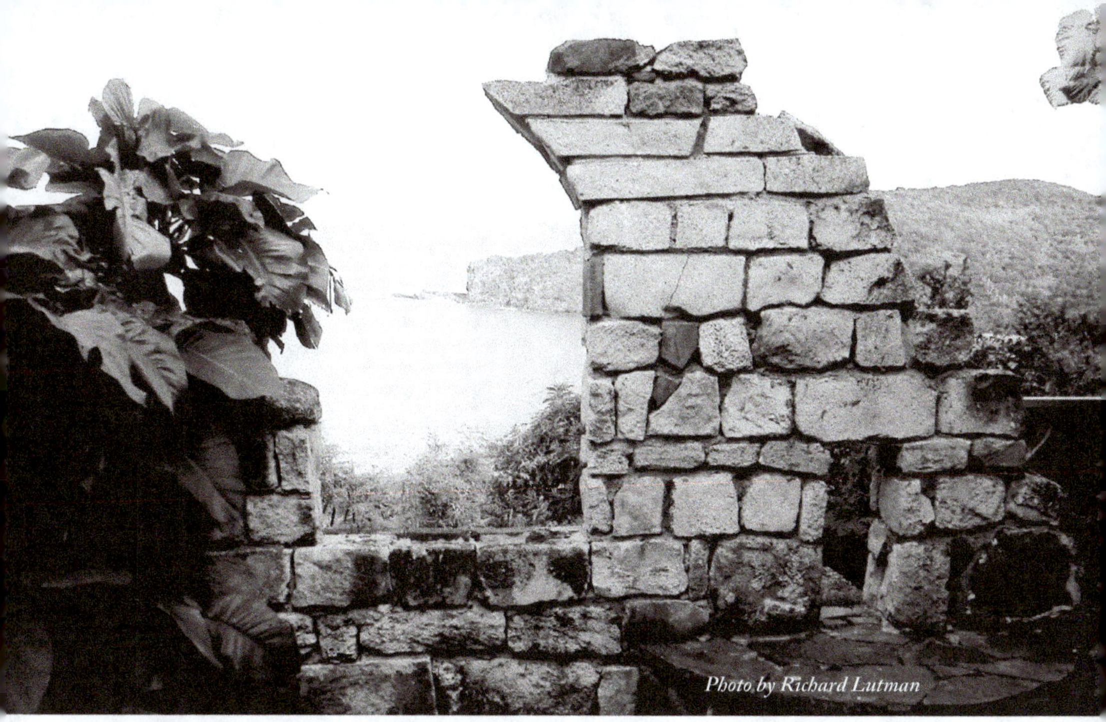

Photo by Richard Lutman

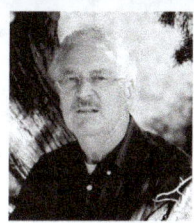

Richard Lutman teaches short story classes as part of Coastal Carolina University's Lifelong Learning program. He has won awards for his short stories, nonfiction, and screenplays. His first novel will be published in 2015.

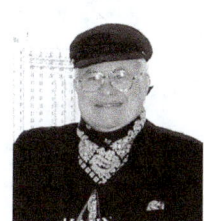

Michael Hugh Lythgoe is a Hoosier by birth. He has lived in Aiken with his wife, Louise, since 2004.

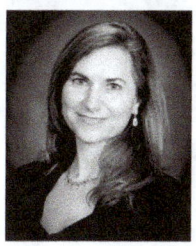

Irena Tervo writes YA, MG, picture books, short stories and articles.